# On Collaboration

# On Collaboration

*Personal, Educational and Societal Arenas*

*By*

Jerry Andriessen and Michael Baker

BRILL
SENSE

LEIDEN | BOSTON

Cover illustration: Drawing by Roxane Oudart-Détienne

All chapters in this book have undergone peer review.

The Library of Congress Cataloging-in-Publication Data is available online at http://catalog.loc.gov

Typeface for the Latin, Greek, and Cyrillic scripts: "Brill". See and download: brill.com/brill-typeface.

ISBN 978-90-04-42906-2 (paperback)
ISBN 978-90-04-42907-9 (hardback)
ISBN 978-90-04-42908-6 (e-book)

Copyright 2020 by Koninklijke Brill NV, Leiden, The Netherlands.
Koninklijke Brill NV incorporates the imprints Brill, Brill Hes & De Graaf, Brill Nijhoff, Brill Rodopi, Brill Sense, Hotei Publishing, mentis Verlag, Verlag Ferdinand Schöningh and Wilhelm Fink Verlag.
All rights reserved. No part of this publication may be reproduced, translated, stored in a retrieval system, or transmitted in any form or by any means, electronic, mechanical, photocopying, recording or otherwise, without prior written permission from the publisher.
Authorization to photocopy items for internal or personal use is granted by Koninklijke Brill NV provided that the appropriate fees are paid directly to The Copyright Clearance Center, 222 Rosewood Drive, Suite 910, Danvers, MA 01923, USA. Fees are subject to change.

This book is printed on acid-free paper and produced in a sustainable manner.

*For Mirjam, Milou, Loek, Vera, Françoise and Éléonore*

Un peu plus, un peu moins, tout homme est suspendu aux récits, aux romans, qui lui révèlent la vérité multiple de la vie.
GEORGES BATAILLE, *Le bleu du ciel* (1957, p. 11)

•••

Ich habe oft geerntet was andere gesät haben, mein Werk ist das eines Kollektivwesens, das den Namen Goethe trägt.
J.W. GOETHE ET AL., *Gespräche: Gesamtausgabe* (1910)

∴

# Contents

**Foreword**   IX
      *Chris Wills and Merisa MacInnes*
**Preface**   XII
**List of Illustrations**   XIV

1   **Introduction**   1
   1   Stories and Principles   3
   2   Why Collaborate?   7
   3   The Structure of This Book   11

2   **Collaboration in Our Lives**   14
   1   Kids' Stuff   14
   2   At School   18
   3   At University   22
   4   PhD and Beyond   25
   5   Main Ideas   31

3   **First Interlude**   34

4   **The Seven Samurai**   38

5   **Spaces for Collaboration**   49

6   **Second Interlude**   55

7   **Collaborating and Learning**   61
   1   A View on Learning   62
   2   Conditions for Collaborative Learning   70
   3   School Learning   73
   4   Summarising Comments on Collaborative Learning   77

8   **Collaborating and Arguing**   83
   1   What Do We Call Argument(ation)?   83
   2   When and Why to Argue   84
   3   What Is the Technique (of Argumentation)?   85
   4   Un-Collaborative Argumentation: Pitfalls   86

5  Argumentation in the Real World: An Illustration   88
  6  Collaborative Argumentation   90
  7  Arguing and Learning   91
  8  Coda   93

9 **How It Feels to Collaborate**   96
  1  An Example of Emotions and Emotional Regulation   97
  2  Diversity and Equality   100
  3  Working towards Shared Goals   101
  4  Considering Other People in Collaboration   102
  5  Epilogue   104

10 **Collaboration and Technology**   107
  1  Collaborative Writing and Technology   109
  2  The Collaborative Working Relationship   111
  3  Collaboration and Technology in Professional Life   114
  4  Bypassing Collaboration   119
  5  Online Media Promoting Collaboration   120
  6  Conclusion: Collaboration and Technology   122

11 **The Principles of Collaboration (How to Do It)**   127

12 **Collaboration: The Warp and Weft of Society**   129
  1  A Participatory View on Society   129
  2  De-Skilling Collaboration   131
  3  Individualistic or Collaborative views on Equality and Sharing   133
  4  The Need for Cooperation   138
  5  Collaborative Practices   140
  6  Coda   143

13 **Aftermath**   153

# Foreword

Long before I [Chris Willis] became an academic, the roots of my interest in collaboration grew in the rich soil of my personal experience of Trade Unionism and the Worker's Co-operative movement in Britain during the late 1970's and early 80's. As one of the youngest elected Shop Stewards in the now defunct National Union of Public Employees, I was an organiser and activist during the early years of Margaret Thatcher's government.

During the term of that Conservative Government's office, I saw first-hand, the effect of policies designed to dismantle Trade Unionism in both the public and private sector, along with the decimation of public services and the destruction of once great and proud industries; but not of the collaborative spirit of the men and women who once worked in them.

The consequent sharp growth in unemployment was one important factor (amongst others) that led to a resurgence of interest in the UK in Producer Co-operation and the formation of Worker's Cooperatives. While many, if not most of the Worker's Co-ops formed in the late 1970's and early 1980's were to fail, a 'new' phenomenon was identified; people collaborating together in co-ops appeared to be demonstratively more 'productive' than in conventionally structured enterprises – and also (seemingly) happier. Although of course, the academic literature from sources as diverse as Marx, Elton Mayo (the "Hawthorne Experiments") and the Tavistock Institute of Human Relations, had long pointed to the importance and benefits of collaboration in both pre-industrial and industrial settings.

"The Productivity Effect of Worker Participation" was the title of my Master's dissertation while a student at Brunel University. The research I undertook for this introduced me to the work of Professor Enid Mumford, who was a leading light in the development of 'participative' approaches to Information Systems Design. This ignited my now life-long interest in participative design, socio-technical systems and the design of computer-based human-activity systems. My interest in 'collaborating' with users in the design of Information Systems has informed, influenced and shaped my career, both as an academic and as a systems analyst. It was in the latter capacity, while working on a large EU-funded project, that I met Jerry Andriessen – and so began another collaboration, during the life-cycle of that project and I am sure, beyond.

While during my career as an academic and a practitioner, I've read many, many dissertations, theses, academic, technical papers and books, *On Collaboration* is the book that I wish that I could have written. Why? – because *On Collaboration* is in and of itself, such a good (and perhaps unique), example of both the narrative approach to describing a process and an exploration of the benefits of collaboration.

We [Chris Wills and Merisa MacInnes] think that this book is important for several reasons. First, and as the authors intended, it leads "an interested reader into reflection and greater understanding of collaboration". This, in itself, is an important contribution, not least because the benefits of collaboration are not widely understood.

Second, as Benjamin Jones (2009) sets out, as technology progresses the knowledge base of individuals becomes, of necessity, more and more specialised. Complex engineering structures, be they hardware or software, have grown and developed to comprise such complexity that for some time now, no single human mind can command a detailed understanding and mastery of such structures. This growth of specialisation as a function of technological complexity drives the need for collaboration as a prerequisite of technological progression. But what is 'collaboration'? How do we/should we/can we 'collaborate'? This book helps the reader reflect upon and begin at least, to understand the nature of collaboration. In doing so, it facilitates and enables the reader's ability better to collaborate in the future.

Third, and echoing the point made by the authors, is that collaboration "concerns people working together as equals". Collaboration is an important key in unlocking creativity – finding solutions to new and unfamiliar problems or creating new artefacts; whether they be works of physical engineering, software or art. Pixar's 'Braintrust' (Catmull & Wallace, 2014) approach to collaborative working is a very good example of highly successful innovative and creative collaborative work. This, despite the fact, that it happens in an 'organised' fashion and is therefore slightly at odds with the authors' clearly expressed view that contrived collaboration can be counterproductive in certain environments. This moreover also, slightly challenges the authors' contention that "the principles of capitalism and hierarchy do not coincide with good collaboration because there is no equality in purposes of different participants ...". Pixar is perhaps the 'exception that proves the rule'.

Finally, we think that this book is important because, as the authors set out in the closing lines of the final chapter:

> Collaboration is not only for the purpose of meeting a challenge. It is the more natural way of relating to others and to the world. It involves looking at the whole instead of beginning from an individualistic perspective. We relate to each other, depend on each other; everything we know and do has been evolving in contexts with others. Creativity comes from relating to others.

This book demonstrates that collaboration is a powerfully productive approach to harnessing the intellectual capital of human kind – we unreservedly recommend that you read it.

### References

Catmull, E., & Wallace, A. (2014). *Creativity Inc.: Overcoming the unseen forces that stand in the way of true inspiration.* New York, NY: Random House. https://doi.org/10.21095/ajmr/2015/v8/i1/88250

Jones, B. F. (2009). The burden of knowledge and the "death of the renaissance man": Is innovation getting harder? *The Review of Economic Studies, 76*(1), 283–317. https://doi.org/10.1111/j.1467-937X.2008.00531.x

*Chris Wills and Merisa MacInnes*
Fowey, Cornwall
August 2019

# Preface

This book presents our exploration of the concept of *collaboration*, as it is given meaning in communal everyday life, including our personal lives, throughout history, in society and in authentic fiction. It is for researchers, although the discourse and tone are not always classically academic. It is for teachers, although it is not always about teaching. It is for journalists, although it is not about journalism. It is an Odyssey even though it is not about Odysseus. It is for anyone who is interested in the esoteric phenomenon called collaboration, and who perhaps wonders why there is so little of it in a world full of people involved in struggling through their individual lives and full of people left alone, stuck in their jobs, or in forgotten places. Such people could perhaps advance in life by gaining a better understanding of how collaborative efforts might well liberate them. At the same time, we do not provide any solutions or scripts for how to do collaboration: our aim is to broaden and deepen thinking, not to constrain and frame it.

As humble researchers we try to explicate the phenomenon of collaboration from various viewpoints, including our own experiences, some of which were scientific experiences. It is our hope that interested readers might be served by viewing collaboration from more than one possible angle, in order to digest and understand collaboration in a richer way, as a phenomenon changing its form and sense every time we try to grasp it. We think that more collaboration in the world would improve the quality of life for many.

The reader should be warned that in this book we express ourselves in different genres, and not only for the sake of adventure. We include stories, fiction, scientific argumentation, explanation, and just enough clarification. It is our conviction that art and fiction, and other genres, may touch and challenge the reader in ways that scientific discourse cannot – our aim is to touch the reader, thereby broadening and deepening the reader's collaboration space.

The authors want to convey their deepest regards for Professor Jay Lemke, who kindly shared with us with his comments on a previous version of the manuscript of this book. As a result, it has much improved. Of course, all content is our own responsibility.

The collective being called Jerry & Michael have harvested ideas sown by many people for more than thirty years. Our thinking on collaboration, learning and technology has benefited from close collaborations with distinguished colleagues, genuinely too numerous to mention: we hope that our citation of at least some of the work of many of them will be considered as an appropriate sign of our indebtedness and wholehearted thanks. More specifically, with respect to the writing of this book and its content, we would like to thank

Mirjam Pardijs and Françoise Détienne for their continual judicious advice. Our thinking on the nature of collaboration presented in Chapter 1 was nourished by our participation in the workshop on "Coordination, Collaboration and Cooperation: Interdisciplinary Perspectives", organised by Federica Amici and Lucas Bietti at the Max Planck Institute for Evolutionary Anthropology, Leipzig, in 2014. Our reflections on argumentation and learning, presented in Chapter 8, owe a great deal to the work of and collaborations with Anne-Nelly Perret-Clermont, Baruch Schwarz and Christian Plantin. Our thinking on affective learning together, in Chapter 9 of this book, was deepened thanks to the European Science Foundation, which financed an exploratory workshop on this theme in 2012. Finally, the majority of our research on technologies for collaboration and learning (see Chapter 10) was carried out thanks to the European Union's financing of several research and development projects in which we participated. On this last point, we express our warmest thanks to our great collaborator and friend, Vittorio Scarano, of the University of Salerno.

# Illustrations

**Figures**

3.1 Rembrandt painting: "The Anatomy Lesson of Dr. Nicolaes Tulp" (1632) (https://upload.wikimedia.org/wikipedia/commons/4/4d/Rembrandt_-_The_Anatomy_Lesson_of_Dr_Nicolaes_Tulp.jpg). 34

3.2 The Garden of Eden with the Fall of Man or The Earthly Paradise with the Fall of Adam and Eve (1617) by Peter Paul Rubens and Jan Brueghel the Elder (https://commons.wikimedia.org/wiki/File:Jan_Brueghel_de_Oude_en_Peter_Paul_Rubens_-_Het_aards_paradijs_met_de_zondeval_van_Adam_en_Eva.jpg). 35

3.3 Mediating artefact (paper) of collaboration between Jerry and Michael on the nature of collaboration. 36

5.1 Scene from the Seven Samurai: Samurai Kikuchiyo with the poor farmers. 49

5.2 "Zu den blauen Flaschen", Vienna Coffeehouse around 1900 (https://commons.wikimedia.org/wiki/File:Zu_den_blauen_Flaschen_painting_c1900.jpg). 51

5.3 A new office space for collaboration (drawing by Roxane Oudart-Détienne). 53

5.4 The authors' collaboration space in summer 2019. 54

6.1 Fun in family board game (drawing by Roxane Oudart-Détienne). 56

6.2 Spectators before a football match (Bradford City versus Plymouth, November 2017). 57

6.3 The wolf pack, protecting itself (drawing by Roxane Oudart-Détienne). 57

6.4 Collaboration in an extreme situation: old farmer lady checking out a Samurai, and vice versa. 58

7.1 The Thinker, Auguste Rodin (1903), symbolising reflection (https://pxhere.com/en/photo/668771). 65

7.2 An ornithography, symbolising intersecting learning trajectories. An ornitography captures in a single time frame the invisible shapes that birds generate when flying, showing their intersecting trajectories. (Picture by Xavi Bou). 69

8.1 Discussing about a humanoid robot of Scarlett Johansson can a be learning experience (drawing by Roxane Oudart-Détienne). 93

10.1 A tool for writing argumentative texts (developed in the 1990s). 109

10.2 A graph depicting deepening of a debate and the relational tensions over time (6 episodes). 114

10.3 Our use of the story to collect experiences with cybercrime. 115

10.4 Tensions (red arrows) between components in the user activity system. 118

ILLUSTRATIONS                                                                XV

10.5   Kids sharing pictures of their breakfast displayed on a digiboard (drawing by Roxane Oudart-Détienne).   121
12.1   Edward Hicks: The Peaceable Kingdom (1834) (https://commons.wikimedia.org/wiki/File:The_Peaceable_Kingdom_by_Edward_Hicks,_c._1846,_oil_on_canvas_-_De_Young_Museum_-_DSC01288.JPG).   135
12.2   Peter Kropotkin c. 1900 (aged 57); Thomas Henry Huxley 1874 (aged 49) (https://en.wikipedia.org/wiki/Peter_Kropotkin and https://en.wikipedia.org/wiki/Thomas_Henry_Huxley).   139

## Table

10.1   Fragment of a chat-discussion between Carla and Betty, on the acceptability of Genetically-Modified Organisms (GMOs).   113

CHAPTER 1

# Introduction

We are both academics. Until recently, our profession was dominated by the model of the individual creator, supposedly some sort of genius working in a mediæval university. Think of Doctor Faustus, alone in his garret room, in a small old German town, poring over heavy, dusty books, staring out of the window, screwing up his face and longing for inspiration to come. And we all know what happened to him.

But the job of research has apparently changed into a more collective, competitive and closely supervised effort. Today, just like everyone else, we spend a lot of time writing big applications for (not necessarily big) finance to carry out joint research projects with other institutions in Europe, the USA and Japan. We analyse data, write papers and books, organise scientific meetings, symposia and the like, with other people; supervise graduate students and manage budgets and are ourselves managed. And we also attend a lot of meetings. But, in the midst of all these common endeavours, the inherent individualism of the job has not changed much. The game still seems to be for each individual to gain personal status and glory (admittedly, in a small world) above others.

But we, the authors of this book, like to collaborate. For example, in writing this book, and others before. It turns out that collaboration is also our research topic. We do research in psychology, education and technology, on how students collaborate and learn by so doing, as well as on how teams collaborate in the workplace. So this book is about collaboration, what it is and when and why it's a good thing to do, across different arenas of life.

We want to show the reader that collaboration is a very rare and precious thing. It is rare because the word 'collaborate' is often used as a kind of smoke screen for hierarchical manipulation. As the French expression goes, the word 'collaboration' has become 'la tarte à la crème', a stodgy yet flashy creamy cake. Much of what is called collaboration is not collaboration. Collaboration is precious because it is vulnerable to various forms of misconduct and misunderstanding. It is rarely explained or taught. Most people do not know how to do it: neither do we, really; which is why we are writing this book.

Should one be given the opportunity to genuinely collaborate, this is a precious gift, for oneself and for others. The world would be a better place if more people collaborated in more areas of life – provided, of course, that they do so for worthy goals. That would exclude, for example, collaborating in order to

© KONINKLIJKE BRILL NV, LEIDEN, 2020 | DOI:10.1163/9789004429086_001 create a totalitarian and repressive state.[1] Certainly, it could be objected that, for some, the ends of totalitarianism – perhaps, increasing the material wellbeing of all, strengthening the nation? – justify the means (repression). In that case, we are obliged to take our stand and to posit as a principle (see below) that collaboration, as we understand it, is linked to *values*, such as equity, mutual respect and not harming others. In that case, this book is not for readers who do not share those values and who believe that authoritarianism, totalitarianism and oppression can be justified.

Collaborating is not just about working together. It is a specific way of working together and relating to others. As we shall explain, *collaborating means developing, in an equal and mutually respectful way, a shared view* of a situation in which people find themselves. Provided it is in the service of making people's lives better, as they see that, we think that collaboration is what we should do more of.

In the rest of this book, we shall gradually refine our idea of what it means to collaborate, as well as the different forms that it can take, drawing on a variety of situations, including some of them excavated from our personal memories. But we need a working definition of collaboration from which to start.

The phrase "what it *means* to collaborate" is a typical expression a social scientist would use. It implies (at least) two things. One, it implies a definition, which is a more or less formal description of what collaboration *is*. But, most importantly, and at the same time, it refers to the experience of collaboration and how this experience is understood, felt, and related to other experiences and social situations.[2] We call this *meaning making*. For example, the experience of collaboration can be understood as important, felt as comfortable, slow, contributing to wellbeing, and many other things. As these are mere concepts, meaning making can also be expressed more holistically. An example of a meaning of collaboration can be found in the comment made by Loek, Jerry's son, then in secondary school: "I do collaboration when the teacher tells me it is useful. However, the assignments are artificial, made up for the purpose of us collaborating. We often do not collaborate equally, some students do a lot of work, others don't do much, or make no attempt at understanding what they should do. Only sometimes it makes sense."

Meaning making is people making sense of themselves, their contexts, and the world. Meanings about collaboration are built up from experiences in various contexts. How people act and react is based on the meanings they have already constructed from previous action.[3]

We would like to tell you two other short stories (there will be a lot of stories in this book).

INTRODUCTION

## 1 Stories and Principles

Recently, there was a feature on the French TV news about the impact on employment of the government's change in policy with respect to employers' social service contributions. Several company directors were interviewed. One of them, a manager of a telephone marketing company, replied as follows: "thanks to the new policy, we have been able to employ many new collaborators". Let's think about the word *collaborator* used by the manager: did it mean anything specific, in that context, or was it just a polite or politically correct way of designating a subordinate employee, who is expected to work hard for the company, and show a high degree of personal motivation? Are the employees also allowed to address their manager as their "collaborator"? After all, people whose job it is to sell products over the telephone work in open-plan offices, each in their own cubicles, with constant surveillance from their manager, assisted by automatic recordings of their conversations. We reply no: this is not collaboration, it is hierarchically structured work, with managers and subordinates; saying that this is 'collaboration' is only a way to dress this up nicely ('tarte à la crème'), and perhaps to say that full involvement is required from workers, in achieving the tasks set by the managers, not the workers. Certainly, people have the right to call things what they like; but in our view, such a loose and even politically strategic use of the word 'collaboration' gets us nowhere.

From this short story we derive a first principle about collaboration, which is that, by definition: *collaboration concerns people who work together as equals.*[4]

'Equal' doesn't mean 'the same' because people are obviously different in many respects, and some of them, such as complementary viewpoints or skills, may be very beneficial to collaboration. But it does mean that people should be *treated* as equals, in terms of mutual *respect* for their views, and that they should be genuinely *free* to say what they think, about the joint task at hand. That freedom has limits of course: those of mutual respect.

Although this first proposal may seem quite obvious, in fact, as we shall discuss in this book, it has far-reaching implications. As we just said, it excludes from collaboration hierarchical situations where people are basically told what to do and have no say in the matter. But, for example, it also implies that traditional teacher-student relations are rarely collaborative in this sense, given that there are no equal rights on each side to criticise what the other does (see Loek's example above). It also means that disagreeing and arguing can be collaborative too, and many more things besides.

Here's a second story, from which we can also get quite a lot of mileage. Around thirty years ago, Michael started working in Lyon (France) as a researcher, just after his PhD. He gave a talk on 'collaborative learning'; and of course, was led to use the words 'collaboration', 'collaborator' and 'collaborative' many times. After the talk, a senior colleague gave him some kindly advice: "if I were you, I'd avoid using the word 'collaboration' here in Lyon; because of the war, when the Germans occupied Lyon, and what happened afterwards to the collabos, it's a word that's very sensitive, with bad associations".

So, what about collaboration in situations of war and invasion? Why were people who went along with the occupying enemy decried as 'collabos'? Why not say they 'cooperated' with the enemy? There is a subtle distinction of meaning between the terms 'collaborate' and 'cooperate', although they both mean working ('labore') or 'operating' together (the 'co-' prefix). To cooperate with the enemy, means to perform certain actions (no doubt under duress, in this case) that go towards achieving the enemy's goals, such as building a defensive ditch. Note that this involves action towards a tangible outcome. But to *collaborate* with the enemy, means to go much further: it is to *actively work on elaborating a shared system of ideas and values* (ideology): and it is *this* way of perceiving people – sharing ideas and values – that brands them as 'collabos'. Cooperation works on the level of action, collaboration also on that of ideas and values.

So, our second principle is that: *collaboration involves people working together to create shared meanings about what they are doing.* Obviously, those ideas do not necessarily concern repressive and repulsive political ideologies. Meanings can concern shared ideas about how to organise a fun end-of-the-year party, or a new chair to be designed, or a lego sculpture, or a maths problem, or even how to live together in shared housing. When they collaborate, people don't just all work separately to achieve a shared objective; they do that, yes; but they discuss whilst doing so, in order to check that they all have more or less the same idea about what they're doing, and even their underlying values.

Let us now return to our two examples, at work, in the telephone marketing call centre, and in education in general, to see how these two principles work out.

In the call centre, the workers – usually women, in fact, since in that line of work they're seen as having better conversational skills and, sadly, many accept to be underpaid – each work in their own cubicles, and the managers oversee what they do. This is some sort of collective enterprise, since all are supposed to have the same goal – selling more products, making more profit for the company, and so on – but it is not collaborative, because: (1) according to the first principle, workers and managers are not all equals, in each being able to contribute with potentially the same repertoire of actions, to how the work is carried out; (2) there is no shared idea being built about how to do the work: the manager tells the workers each what to do. And so, in a sense, there is a 'shared idea': but it is one that the workers cannot co-create; they are simply required to 'share' the idea imposed on them by the boss. So what is important is that both principles 1 and 2 are satisfied *together*: (principle 1) all can freely contribute (principle 2) to the elaboration of the shared idea, rather than each being required to 'swallow' or even actively contribute to the idea of a single authority.

What would a collaborative version of this be like? That's quite simple. There would be regular meetings during which all telephone operators, managers, everyone concerned, share their experiences of what worked and what didn't, and where a new idea of what to do to make the work more effective is elaborated *together*. And collaboration would no doubt go further, to concern how to make the work more satisfying, less painful for each and equally remunerated ....

Collaboration, like love, cannot be imposed. The equality principle asks for two-way or multiparty interactions, beginning from the will to collaborate. Whilst it would seem strict to only include spontaneous collaboration as the genuine experience, it makes sense to prefer instances of collaboration where all participants more or less agree about doing it.

We cannot escape the fact that collaboration has a set of underlying *values*. It's about respecting people, and not only about freely co-creating shared ideas about joint projects. It is probably worth formulating this as a third principle: *collaboration is a way of working together that involves mutual respect for the dignity, the feelings, the person, the lifeworld, the experience of all concerned.*

We just mentioned that the call centre workers would have regular meetings, to build a better idea together of what they're trying to do. But just a minute: meetings take time, obviously; and we can already hear the objection "collaboration is a waste of time, it would be more efficient and profitable to manage people and tell them what to do" ... so the objection might go. Yes: *collaboration takes time*. But who says it's less efficient, in the long run? Of course, in the short term, meetings take time. But the shared ideas, feelings of being respected and on the same wavelength, may be a good 'investment' for the future. People who are happy and less stressed work better, and probably more efficiently.[5] We shall return to this issue – why collaborate? – later in the book.

Let us now turn to education, schools and universities. The same issues come up: efficiency, values, respect for others. It seems that most educational systems and practices are based on the idea that it's somehow more 'efficient' for the teacher to race through the right answers in front of the students, on the black or white board, the PowerPoint slides; for the students to swallow and retain; and that getting students to work in groups, to collaborate, is somehow less efficient. This is the model of the teacher who holds authority and truth, with the students there to suffer and absorb it. Obviously, we strongly disagree, on several counts. Knowledge that you created and understood yourself, with others, is not at all the same as information transmitted by the teacher, that you memorised (and later forgot). It's as simple as that; and we shall return to this point again and again in this book.

There's another thing that will sometimes pop up: is collaboration a 'natural' way of behaving? Or are we all individuals, only there to fully develop ourselves at any cost? Or to say it in a more principled way: don't we start as social individuals, being better at collaboration than at individual action[6]? Who hasn't witnessed small children, alone at first, not knowing what to do, immediately springing into action when becoming part of a small group?

And again, who says that, on a broader scale, that of society, that we would not all benefit, in the long run, from producing people who think for themselves but with others? Isn't that what the post-knowledge society is all about? Innovation? The collaborative society is coming and we should embrace it. It is people who respect each other, work with each other, and like doing that who are the makers and guardians of our future. Knowledge gained from collaboration is just more creative and oriented towards the future.

It is time to sum up and move on. We said that, as a fair first pass, collaboration is an activity that is carried out in accordance with at least the three following principles,[7] whereby people:
- (principle 1) work together as *equals*;
- (principle 2) *develop shared meaning* about what they are doing;
- (principle 3) *show consideration* for each other.

In the rest of this book, we shall extend and deepen these principles in several ways, drawing on a variety of sources, including personal memories, scientific research on collaboration, and even fiction films. Many stories will be told here, because we like stories; but also because according to the very influential educational psychologist, Jerome Bruner, storytelling, or narrative, is a distinctive mode of human existence, or way of understanding the world, different from scientific rationality.

Our aims in this book are simple: to cut through media hype on collaboration and provide a more clear and useful idea of what collaboration is and is not, arguing that life would be better if we all collaborated. But before dealing with these issues, in an attempt to motivate some readers, we address the question: *why collaborate?*

## 2   Why Collaborate?

Why collaborate? Why do anything at all? Why eat vegetables, love your children, pay your debts, or vote for the socialist candidate? It seems that there are five main related ways to answer such questions.

First, deciding to do something or not can be considered in terms of the *consequences* of that action: being healthy, being loved in return, receiving credit in the future, improving wellbeing for all, etc.

Second, you might choose to do something in order to conform to *rules*, such as of ethics or law: parental responsibility, respecting contracts with banks or being a responsible democratic citizen.

Third, you might simply do something because it is coherent with your *values*: respecting animal rights, promoting equality in society, and so on.

Fourth, you might do something simply *unthinkingly*, because that is what you do or who you are: because other people do that, because that was the way you were brought up, or because you were told or constrained to do it.

Fifth, and finally, you might collaborate because you realise that you have *no choice* but to do that! "Collaborate or lose, die, etc.", we might say. This is about choice between alternatives, each of which are supposed to be clearly understood (collaborate and survive, win, gain, or else die, lose). Concentration camps, during the Second World War, comprised hundreds of thousands, millions, of brutalised starved prisoners and a few hundred guards. If the prisoners had collaborated, they could have overrun the guards, probably at the 'price' of death of hundreds of the prisoners. Of course, this is reasoning carried out by healthy, free, well-fed people, not that of people who had been systematically deprived of freedom, well-being, dignity and even their status as human beings. Nevertheless, thinking as an individual, the question is, will it be me who survives or dies? Thinking collaboratively, one wants the general aim of freedom of the group. Collaboration, in extreme circumstances, requires a leap of faith in the success of the joint venture, and decentralisation from oneself as an individual.

We have nothing to say here about the fourth reason, other than that we would hope that society in general would become more collaborative over historical time, and thus collaborating more would become second nature to people. And this could, in terms of the second reason, become a social practice sanctioned by rules. And of course, the fifth reason is a very clear case, even though it is not always clear to people that they have no real choice but to collaborate, which relates to the fifth reason (having no choice but to collaborate), about which another book could be written, and has been, no doubt. Luckily, most opportunities for collaboration are not extreme in this way. There is the problem of people being able to see, to be convinced by, the aims for all, or nearly all, of collaboration.

So we will think about the first and third reasons for doing something: *consequences* and *values*. What are the consequences, for the individual, others, society and humanity as a whole, of becoming more collaborative, and what are the underlying values? Of course, if someone does not wish for or accept the consequences, or rejects the associated values, nothing can be said. We can only try to lay them out, and invite people to accept or reject them.

The values associated with collaboration are the easiest aspect to deal with. They are incorporated in our working definition of collaboration, presented in this chapter, above: a preference for interacting with others as equals, for working to build something together, instead of building it alone and asking others to take it on, and for mutual consideration. These are the values of equality, of being and working together in mutual respect. In some way, these values are 'take it or leave it'. We think that most people would be ashamed to openly admit that they do not subscribe to these values of collaboration – that would be tantamount to admitting that one is an individualist who cares little for others. Sure: it can be a matter of degree.

So, let's look at the possible *consequences* of the collaborative way of living, and the reader can choose. To say it another way: what would the collaborative world or life be like?

*To collaborate is to be human.* Many researchers, such as the group of Michael Tomasello at Max Planck Institut, Leipzig, consider that it is our ability to *collaborate* that distinguishes us from other primates, in addition to vastly more elaborate capacities for language, social organisation and production of tools. And in fact, all these go together: advanced social organisation is required for producing tools, killing beasts, cooking and eating them; and the more the organisation is complex, the more it requires communication for coordinating it. Chimpanzees do hunt effectively in groups. But they seem to each grab a part of the jointly caught prey, with little sign of collaborating to share it. Although some do give up their food to others, it is not clear that this comes from altruism rather than from fear of being bitten if they don't concede. What makes us specifically human is our ability to collaborate, and this involves social organisation, technology and communication in dialogue. Collaboration is not only operational, however: it seems that we have a *drive* towards it, in some sense for its own sake.[8] It's called being social. A child could play many games alone; but it's more rewarding to play together, to feel part of a group, to not be alone or excluded. (Not always, of course: it depends on the others involved in the game). Rather than solving problems at their own desk

INTRODUCTION 9

in school, most children would prefer to work on them in small groups. It's human, and often feels good.

*Collaboration is a specific, often rewarding experience.* You might want to collaborate in order to have that experience. Collaboration usually involves dialogue, unless people have perfect knowledge of each other, and are doing something together that they each know by heart. Merleau-Ponty described the experience of dialogue – and the same goes for collaboration – as follows:

> In the experience of dialogue, a common ground is created between the other and myself, my thinking and that of the other make up only one woven cloth, my comments and those of the interlocutor are called forth by the state of the discussion; they insert themselves into a common operation of which none of us is the creator.[9] (Our translation from the original French)

This sounds a bit like the 'flow experience',[10] when you feel outside yourself, the piece of music, the painting, the problem, that are playing, painting, solving themselves in some way. It's a good experience! And being able to have such an experience supposes a willingness to dissolve oneself in the joint enterprise. Not everyone accepts to do that – many prefer to dominate and try to have their own way. But then they won't have the collaborative experience; in some sense, such people are less 'human' than others.

But of course, working in groups is not always enjoyable. That is because it is often *not* collaborative, in terms of our principle of mutual consideration. Sure, other people can be annoying, and not show you respect. But they will do so if, as we define it, they collaborate with you.

*If you collaborate, you can do things that you could not do alone.* This is obvious in the case of large-scale projects such as building a house, or a bridge. You might be able to do that alone, but you probably don't have all the requisite skills, and it would take a very long time: one reason why you need to collaborate is because, physically, the task can't be done alone. In many small communities, including Italian and Portuguese immigrants in the outskirts of Paris during the 1950s, in fact people grouped together to build the house of one family with their own hands, then moved on to the others' houses. That's not just more practical, collaborating also builds the sense of belonging to a community.

But there is another reason why collaborating enables you to do things you could not do alone, which is that the products of collaboration are in some way *special*, in comparison with solo products. They have a special ring to them; they are in some way more general, and generally accepted, because they have already stood up to the test of the group. If we think of art, painting, music, literature, over the past two or three millennia, it is almost always a case of the individual genius (in Chapter 3 we mention a rare exception in the case of the painting 'Adam and Eve', by Rubens and Bruegel). Why aren't there more collaborative novels, paintings and string quartets? And what would such collaborative art forms be like? Rock music is sometimes written by the group. But record sleeve notes usually indicate that one or two musicians take the credits. Designing a large building usually requires a team of architects; but there again, it is usually the boss who takes the credit. We don't really know why there are so few collaborative works of art in this world. We seem to be still living in a world that wants to create heroes, 'Great Men' of the nineteenth century. Below we will try to speculate about what a collaborative world would look like.

All the things that we have listed above, concerning what you can get out of collaboration, can also be obtained by the other people who have worked with you. Inclusion in the group, a valuable experience, extending your thinking beyond yourself, doing things you could not do alone. Why *not* collaborate? If you don't like other people, if you want to take credit for yourself, if you want to be alone, ...?

Now; what about the group, society, rather than oneself? What would the collaborative world look like?

Let's first deal with an obvious question: efficiency. In many circumstances, such as in the army, the factory and the hospital, it is seen as more efficient to have a clear hierarchy of command, with clear individual responsibilities. But as everyone knows, the frenetic chase towards higher production, economic growth, is depleting the world's resources, and destroying it. Efficiency, even if it is demonstrated in the above cases – which is not certain, given the existence of viable cooperatives – is not and should not be the only criterion. The question is: what is the world in which we can all live and want to live in? In this case, we introduce a second criterion, which is *how* do we want to live together? In a capitalist world of Ford-like production, or in a world where we collaborate? Or some combination of the two? In the collaborative world, some people will perhaps not get so rich; but most will be quite happy and well fed. Apart from cases of very poor countries, there is enough to go round, so that we can all live and preserve our world. People have tried to evaluate 'happiness' in different countries. It seems that an important factor is not so much the average income, but the *difference* between incomes: people are unhappy when they compare themselves to others, not always because of their individual circumstances *per se*.

"This is communism", some might say. But it is not: it is about a world in which we create wellbeing for all by collaborating more. And collaboration can only be carried out in relatively small groups, where all can interact, respect and understand each other. There could be no such state ideology as 'collaborativism'. On the level of society, it is a matter of encouraging people to group together on a more local basis, to live, produce and create. A more collaborative world would create more wellbeing all round.

## 3   The Structure of This Book

In the next chapter (Chapter 2), "Collaboration in our lives", we delve into our pasts, across family, leisure, school and work, to try to find clear and good examples of collaborations in which we participated. It turns out that such experiences were rare, so we reflect on the conditions that are necessary for collaboration to be possible. We then return, in Chapter 3, as we shall do several times, to refining the concept of collaboration. In Chapter 4, we analyse a film, *The Seven Samurai*, by Akira Kurosawa, one of the most referred to and remade films in the history of cinema, that gives an example of the necessity of collaboration in order to survive. We then examine, in Chapter 5, the different physical and social spaces that may or may not favour collaboration. This is followed, as we said it would, by another return to lessons learned for the idea of collaboration, in Chapter 6. Chapters 7 to 9 deal with specific topics relating to collaboration, on which we have done research in the past. In Chapter 7, we discuss how collaboration, as a process of co-creation of ideas, can be important for learning.

It might be thought that collaboration involves always agreeing with each other: we show, in Chapter 8, that specific ways of arguing about issues together can be supremely collaborative.

From our principles stated above, it might sound as if collaboration is just about creativity and ideas. It is about that, but, as we discuss in Chapter 9, collaboration is a particular shared experience, associated with particular emotions that in turn influence the way things go.

In previous decades, there was a wealth of work on how 'new technologies' influenced our lives, probably because they did in some way represent a break with the past. But today, technology is a part of everyone's lives: in a way, it is 'normal'. In Chapter 10 we discuss the way that technology has created new opportunities for collaboration, and also for pseudo-collaboration.

We return again, in Chapter 11, to take stock of how far we have come in understanding collaboration, and to provide some brief answers to the question: how should you collaborate? We claim that it is not just a matter of doing things more efficiently together than alone, although the jury is still out on whether collaboration is more or less efficient than the individualist way, but rather that it is a choice of a way of life, and one that everyone who wants a better life for all should take.

In Chapter 12, we broaden the discussion to look at the extent to which collaboration, as it has so far been defined, is gradually coming to the fore in society.

What could we conclude, in Chapter 13, other than that collaboration is what we should do?

We hope that you enjoy this book as much as we have enjoyed collaborating in writing it.

### Notes

1. See Drapac and Pritchard (2017).
2. See Crook (1994).
3. See Schwartz (1999).
4. See Baker (2015).
5. See Oswald, Proto, and Sgroi (2015); Ledford (1999) and Seppälä (2016).
6. See Vygotsky (2012).
7. Inspired by Roschelle and Teasley (1995); Dillenbourg (1999); and Baker (2015).
8. See Crook (1994).
9. See Merleau-Ponty (1945, p. 407).
10. See Csikszentmihályi (1990).

### References

Baker, M. J. (2015). Collaboration in collaborative learning. *Interaction Studies: Social Behaviour and Communication in Biological and Artificial Systems, 16*(3), 451–473. https://doi.org/10.1075/is.16.3.05bak

Crook, C. (1994). *Computers and the collaborative experience of learning*. London: Routledge.

Csikszentmihályi, M. (1990). *Flow: The psychology of optimal experience*. New York, NY: Harper & Row.

Dillenbourg, P. (Ed.). (1999). *Collaborative learning: Cognitive and computational approaches*. Amsterdam: Pergamon/Elsevier Science.

Drapac, V., & Pritchard, G. (2017). *Resistance and collaboration in Hitler's empire*. London: Macmillan International Higher Education.

Ledford, G. E. (1999). Comment: Happiness and productivity revisited. *Journal of Organizational Behavior, 20*, 25–30.

Merleau-Ponty, M. (1945). *Phénoménologie de la perception*. Paris: Gallimard (Collection TEL).

Oswald, A. J., Proto, E., & Sgroi, D. (2015). Happiness and productivity. *Journal of Labor Economics, 33*(4), 789–822.

Roschelle, J., & Teasley, S. D. (1995). The construction of shared knowledge in collaborative problem solving. In C. O'Malley (Ed.), *Computer supported collaborative learning* (pp. 69–97). Berlin: Springer-Verlag.

Schwartz, D. L. (1999). The productive agency that drives collaborative learning. In P. Dillenbourg (Ed.), *Collaborative learning: Cognitive and computational approaches* (pp. 197–218). Amsterdam: Elsevier.

Seppälä, E. (2016). *The happiness track: How to apply the science of happiness to accelerate your success*. London: Hachette UK.

Vygotsky, L. S. (2012). Thought and language (Rev. and Expanded ed.). Cambridge, MA: The MIT Press.

CHAPTER 2

# Collaboration in Our Lives

After having given a first sketch of collaboration, in this chapter we now explore situations in which collaboration may happen, from the perspective of personal experience. We narrate some of our experiences with successful or failed collaboration in our lives so far. As we were born in 1960 (Michael) and in 1956 (Jerry), these lives already are quite long. By discussing collaboration in this way, we do not define it as an abstraction, but rather start from experience, bringing out collaboration and the situational aspects that seem to be linked it, facilitating or limiting collaboration, insofar as we reconstruct our experience, from memory, for the purposes of this book. One lesson to be learned here is that every situation is entirely different, and ideal collaboration, as an idealisation, will be quite different in practice. Our aim here is to increase understanding of the nature of collaboration, not to tell people how to be perfect collaborators.

We, the two authors of this book, have worked together for a long time, around thirty years. We're both academics, did our PhDs in Psychology (Jerry) and Cognitive Science (Michael) around thirty years ago. We both work on collaborative learning: trying to understand how students work together in order to learn. We began to work together first talking about things we were both interested in, over a few beers, then doing concrete research projects, designing and making software for schools, with funding from the European Community. Quite intense, stressful experiences. But it's been a good experience, we agree. We have become good friends and have enjoyed working together. We have a few stories to tell about how we worked together, including in the writing of this book, that will come to the surface throughout it. But each of us has our own stories to tell, about memorable, good and bad experiences when we had to do things with others.

## 1      Kids' Stuff

*Jerry:*   I recall collaboration during play: building huts, tents, sandcastles together with the kids next door. Huts were big, more kids would fit into them, and there was no negotiation on how they were built, or not much. New additions held out, or they did not. That's how we worked, by adding stuff to an existing artefact. I remember being quite bossy. This was because I was the oldest. When an older, or stronger child played with us, I was more modest, and tried to ally with the strong one. Kids not in the group were enemies, kids known to some of us but not all (e.g. cousins or classmates) could join in, but had to behave. Did we always agree and were we always considerate? Probably not, we could have fierce arguments and adults had to intervene. In my memory it usually was a lack of attention and consideration by (some) others that caused (part of) the group to diverge or stop doing hut building with the others.

Play can be taken as an active form of learning and communication: kids of different ages grow to understand and like each other (and other things) by playing together. Often this already is collaborative. During natural play,[1] children synchronise their efforts in some way, and there is some spontaneous division of roles. All kids contributed to building the hut, according to their capabilities. This house building game is a culturally-historically transmitted activity, that exists across different cultures – Michael also did the same play hut building in England, rather than in the Netherlands, at the beginning of the 1960s. The goal of playing together was in the activity itself: being together and being involved in a joint and pleasant activity. Joint in the sense of together working on (the same or different parts of) the same artefact, as well as sharing the same goal, albeit not knowing exactly in advance what the outcome will be, only that it matches some general idea. Pleasant in the sense of kids behaving considerately if they can, until that breaks down for some reason, and then they make it up or split up. We can say that the term collaboration qualifies an aspect (or type) of play, and it emerges naturally from social and emotional interests.

In childhood, we collaborate with other children on the basis of friendship, similarity and joint interests. Collaboration may take the form of some division of leadership roles. There are culturally inscribed formats of collaboration that are passed down from generation to generation.

*Michael:* In my childhood, apart from the play hut building the only collaboration I can remember was with a friend who lived opposite; he played piano, I played classical guitar. Each of us would come round to the other's house with an idea, a chord sequence, a short theme. Cassette player up on the piano, busking through a few times, then we'd record. It felt great listening to what we had done. Not that it was of excellent musical value. But it was music of sorts; and we had made it, made something, together. That justified a lot of coffee with milk, and biscuits (before we graduated to beer). He now is a composer. And I'm writing this book with Jerry.

This was collaboration; both could play, would comment and give suggestions on each other's play. Michael's friend was pretty bossy, though, Michael thought he was not very flexible, he wanted to be right. We were more or less equal in ability, as boys of fourteen, but there was competition, at least from one side. There was not always real equality in actual collaboration. There were tensions in that the friend was concerned about being the best.

It seems that collaboration can have some competition in it as well, actual or felt, when one participant is bossier than the other, or when one participant tries to be the better one. We have to learn how to deal with (manifested) differences in temperament, talent, and motivation. These differences can be sources of tension, but can also (and at the same time) be very productive.

Making music seems to be an excellent example of collaboration, or at least, of joint creativity.[2] But it also may be merely cooperative. For example, the history of the band called Soft Machine, as narrated by its former member Robert Wyatt,[3] shows us that the members of the band were very different in character, did not like each other very much, and had different views about music. When they were not playing, the band members were on their own. Playing together went quite well, the band was very successful in its time. What does that imply for equality, mutual respect and sharing the goal of making (some kind of) good music? What probably counts is that the group members offered each other the opportunity for playing together, which was sufficiently satisfying, personally, and as a group, but for several different reasons. At the moments when they performed, the musicians shared the goal of making music, respecting each other's contributions, fine tuning to what the others were doing (which is a highly sensitive skill, although there are different standards for such sensitivity), this may well go as far as collaboration can. People can learn to deal with certain differences, especially when they move forward collaboratively. Most studio music albums and songs, especially famous ones, are not the result of synchronous collaboration, as in playing together at the same time, at all. Band members contribute individually to a multi-track recording on tape, and the final result is then edited by an expert technician.[4]

*Jerry:* At home, I used to watch my father create a miniature railway for me and my younger brother. He did all the work, and we bonded by me being present. There were some small and insignificant negotiations about tracks and the presence of cars where I recall having had some influence on the proceedings. My father thought aloud with me present during the activity, and I may have learned a thing or two. I was interested, wanted to do what he did and how he did it, tried to understand why, but he achieved the perfection that I never could, or could even attempt. It was about being clever with your hands and slowly advancing in building up an artificial empire. We also collaborated in collecting stamps: I did the bookkeeping, he did the acquisitions, and gradually I was allowed to take over putting the stamps into neat albums. Our collection of national stamps was nearly complete, with the exception of the most expensive ones. Although my interest was long over, my father continued the acquisition of new stamps and re-created the process with my (11-year) younger brother. After my father's death I now own two nearly complete (until the mid-nineteen-nineties) collections of Dutch national stamps.

*Michael:* I remember trying to work with my father. Or rather, trying to help him with his work. When I say work, I really mean work: he was a car mechanic, when I was around ten years old – his way of escaping from the coal mines. In the evenings, after work, he fixed old cars that no-one else wanted, so that we could have a car. I can remember that in the cold months of the year, in the north east of England, my mother would sometimes push me out of the door, telling me to go and help my father. He was usually lying on his back under the car, parked in the street, on an old army blanket (the cold ground must have crept through), oil falling onto his face, grunting and cursing and clinking as he worked. Hearing me say hello Dad, he would just call out for a particular tool, a spanner, a wrench, screwdriver, of a specific size, that I had to pass to him. He was the master: I was the apprentice. Then, under the bonnet of the car, he would tweak, twiddle with things. I would ask him to explain what he was doing, or to tell me what was the part he was working on. But he seemed so concentrated on the problem (it seemed to take a lot of effort) that he couldn't or simply didn't explain: he would just ask me to hold something, or to pass him something. Then it was over. It was not collaboration. Of course, I didn't know anything. But he didn't explain anything. I just became cold. The truth is, I didn't really want to be out there with him. Perhaps he was pleased I was there anyway, but he never showed it. He fixed radio sets too. Once he explained to me about valves. And then, about the new invention: transistors. But the truth is, I wasn't very interested in that, his passion, electrical circuits.

Michael and his father did not collaborate. What would have made it collaboration? Even if there was a complete difference in skill in car mechanics, they could nevertheless go for a master-apprentice relationship.[5] Something they both liked doing seemed important. Being interested in engines and electrical circuits could have meant Michael leaving school early to become a technician, whereas he knew he wanted to stay at school as long as possible. His father tried taking an interest in geology (collecting rocks and fossils), which Michael was interested in, but his father didn't succeed in becoming interested. Jerry and his dad did not really collaborate either in building the artefact together. Both Jerry and Michael participated simply by being present, looking at what Dad did. Jerry was *interested* but passive. When he was allowed to become more active, it was by division of work rather than collaboration. How would it be possible to collaborate in collecting stamps? Maybe by going to meetings together, or to see colleagues who had a lot of stamps for sale (we actually did that); or by deepening understanding of the pictures on the stamps during discussion (we did not). It could involve joint diagnosis of the quality of some exemplar, or joint reading and commenting on a collection including our own (we did not).

Liking each other, being co-present, even having a shared interest in the making of the artefact, seem insufficient alone for collaboration to take place. On the other hand, joint work on the artefact is possible without liking or even joint interest. Collaboration situations have their social and emotional prerequisites. At least in the old days, the relationships between fathers and sons were too complicated, and far from equal to be able to lead to collaboration.

## 2    At School

*Jerry:* My mother contributed to the family income as a typist. I loved the typewriters that we had at home. At primary school, sixth grade, I started my own journal, writing about made-up sports events with my classmates as heroes and heroines. Also, because the teacher loved it (he liked me), many classmates wanted to contribute to the journal. When they came with stories, I altered them completely and only kept their name as an author. The interviews were especially successful. I made up a set of questions and the journalist went and had an interview (with a classmate or teacher) and wrote down the answers. Sometimes he added one or two funny questions and answers, which I then kept. There were no editorial meetings: I was the guy with the typewriter. We are talking late sixties now.

This is interesting, since it is an experience with organising a collaborative enterprise: making a journal. There was not even a hint of joint effort or even a joint discussion. There was one boss (Jerry), owning the means of production, including the press, delegating small tasks to the others. It resembled a capitalist economy, and probably many organisations still function in this way. The bosses and the workers do not share common interests, beyond the continued existence of the enterprise, and workers rarely join forces and collaborate, such as in meetings discussing how to do the work better, or to change working conditions. As in Jerry's journalism example, workers who disagree with or dislike the boss are ignored or simply thrown out.

In a capitalist economy, where the bosses own the means of production, they also tend to decide everything. Capitalism and collaboration do not match, probably because there is no equality of power and interest.

*Michael:* During all my schooling: no collaboration with anyone. We were mostly all at our separate desks, no talking allowed, standing up to attention when the masters entered the room. It was only in the science lab that we in some way had to work together (there wasn't enough apparatus for each kid). I can't remember really talking much with the other kids I worked with: we were under pressure to finish the experiment in time, to understand what the teacher asked us to do. It was not about understanding what the other thought about the experiment: just a matter of doing it quickly and right.

*Jerry:* Also, I remember collaborating with a friend in doing a funny play for the teacher's birthday: I was the machine, hidden inside a large box, and my friend was the professor, who invented the box and could communicate with it. We both contributed to the script, I guess.

There is a clear difference between collaboration and being asked to do a task together. This has to do with a lack of an authentic need to solve a problem, but even more with a lack of necessity to join forces and for understanding each other. Even leisure activity can be more collaborative than school-work. When are joint products really relevant in schools? Is working together to each deliver an individual report a sufficient motive for collaboration?

*Jerry:* In secondary school, in the final two years (age 16), I was part of a group of boys who produced a journal. No bosses anymore, all of us were equal, albeit some were better in drawing while others stuck to writing. We had editorial meetings, with beer and cigarettes, during which we jointly produced modern texts arguing against monarchy, government, establishment, and against teachers in particular.

> The journal was declared illegal and we were nearly kicked out of school, especially because of the very naturalistic illustrations. Some of us also made music together, most of it improvised, and we called it jazz. This was the early seventies. We each played all instruments that we could get hold of, and any contribution was valid, although not always appreciated by all. Sometimes you could hear one musician trying to make himself heard by others, by repeating some phrases, or by playing loudly, which could be picked up or not.

Neither the quality of the journal, nor that of our music was of any concern. These are different forms of collaboration, not aiming for artefact production, and maybe not even joint activity, but further discovery of the self in relation to others and the world. These were social endeavours during which various forms of violating social norms were exercised. It could be termed 'relational collaboration', mediated by drawings, text and musical sound.

There probably are phases in human development during which particular aspects of collaboration are acquired and elaborated by goal-directed activities. Dealing with the external world (interaction) in relation to the incentive dimension (mental balance and sensitivity to others) is probably part of early adolescence.

*Michael:* In the two years before the exams at age eighteen (called 'A levels', in England), they had forced me to do maths and science: because I was a boy (I still am, in my late fifties) and I could in fact do maths. There was no collaboration in maths classes either; but the teacher didn't prevent us from talking to our neighbours. I was quite ok at maths, but I made the mistake of really trying to understand the problem, instead of just doing it. I remember the boy I sat next to: a real social misfit, what we called then a 'drongo" (he didn't have a girlfriend, of course). As an adult, he became an economist. The teacher wrote out the problem to be solved, then indicated, in the back of the book, special 'exhibition' questions (from a national competitive examination), for those detestable boys who had solved the problem so quickly that they had nothing else to do. My neighbour thought about nothing: he simply immediately and quickly wrote out the solution to the problem. Then he went on to do a couple of exhibition questions, out of boredom. Meanwhile, I worked through the question, screwing up my eyes, just in time. I peeked at what my neighbour had written, but that did not help. "But how do you do it, Ian?", I asked, many times. He looked at me, nonplussed: "but it's obvious, isn't it? You just write out the answer ...". He couldn't explain. No collaboration there.

The teacher did not ask us to collaborate, although he did not forbid it either. You could talk to your neighbours, and look at his exercise book. Copying was forbidden, however. Not being able to explain what you have done (in order to correctly solve a maths exercise) suggests complete absence of understanding. We were all teenage boys, without exception, in that maths class in the mid-1970s. It is quite possible that girls collaborate more and more effectively.

One advantage of collaboration could be learning to understand what others do or being able to explain to others how we understand things. Both seem to be crucial qualities for sharing understanding and learning in general.[6] Apparently successful school careers do not require this, or at least they didn't in the seventies. Michael's drongo classmate was not able to explain anything: he simply solved all of the most difficult maths problems (even the teacher had difficulties with some of them) without being able to say how or why. If knowledge remains individual, there is not much to be shared, and collaboration is obviously futile. Would it still be possible in today's society to pass school exams without having experienced the need for collaboration? It probably is.

*Jerry:* Was there any collaboration at school, about school tasks, or during lessons? I do not think so. Before the final exam, a friend and I worked together on solving physics problems, and genuinely tried to explain to each other how we worked things out. We were not desperate at needing to understand everything, but we were eager to pass the exam. I was a poor student, because I did not care about school. I was a good student because I achieved success with minimal effort. Working together was evidence of liking school, which was not done in our little subgroup. So, we did not tell. Why did we hate school? My idea is that it was because we did not feel noticed as individuals. Those who were noticed as individuals by the system did not have more to offer than the system they confirmed; so in our eyes they were slaves and Pharisees, being friendly with the enemy.

Group norms and tensions, caused by interacting with people who are not part of the group, can prevent collaboration even being considered. Because such issues tend to remain unresolved, they may recur as intergroup conflicts even at an adult age. This relates to the specific connotation of collaboration as 'working with the enemy', in particular during World War II (see Chapter 1 of this book). Essentially, these are issues of the self in relation to the world;

and the learning process during adolescence should address sensitivity as well as mental balance with respect to group differences and our individual roles in groups.[7] We suggest creating various collaborative activities (as in 'sensitivity' training) to achieve such balance, especially during adolescence. And yes, we should learn to work with the enemy, but perhaps less so during wartime.

The period of human development characterised by finding an identity within and against groups of people makes collaboration hard with those who are not a part of the group. Designing collaborative activities with the aim of finding out ways of handling relational tensions, developing knowledge or skill in dealing with differences, would be a possible (albeit probably imposed) solution.

## 3   At University

*Jerry:* During the first years at University (Psychology) we had lectures and tutorial groups. Quite a lot of those groups, in which 10–20 students answered questions, discussed lectures and listened to presentations. I soon only attended the most essential lectures and avoided the workgroups, because you had to speak and discuss, and I did not feel at ease in discussing things I did not understand with people I did not know very well. During the same period, I had long discussions with my friends, about things we did not understand at all, had beers, played music, and went to every concert and movie that we found interesting.

It appeared that, at least in the Netherlands in the seventies, university education was not lecturing alone. The tutorial group was invented long before – allegedly, by Wilhelm von Humboldt[8] – as a way of discussing course content, on the basis of exercises such as summary presentations, presenting issues for discussion, by the students. The setup was not collaborative at all; each student came with individual questions and issues. Maybe at some points, some discussion (for example, argumentative discussion: see Chapter 8 of this book) would happen; but with the teacher present, the main goal was finding correct interpretations to poorly understood parts of the course. Those who felt they could get away with it did not attend.

*Jerry:* At University, there was one group obligation during the 3-year bachelor period that could not be avoided, called 'The Project'. The project involved a period of several months (two days a week) during which a group of ten students collaborated on a research project of their own choice. As a group, we knew each other already from spending time together under the same mentor. During The Project we conducted interviews, looked for coaches and experts, developed a questionnaire, did statistical analyses, jointly analysed and interpreted outcomes, and produced a report. In contrast to earlier experiences with collaboration, here we met once a week, had long discussions and shared most of what we did. Although I tried, I could not remain a backbencher, and got some responsibilities to fulfil, alone or with others. Gradually, my personal meaning-making shifted from avoiding responsibility towards joint participation and meaning-making.

This was one of the most collaborative experiences at university. I think many of the participants in the project did learn a lot, they were the most involved ones, probably motivated both by their interest in the topic and by working together. The project clearly was collaborative in the sense that we addressed each other's work and were open for criticism. In the spirit of this project we all agreed we were beginners, and there were no differences in expertise to worry about, only differences in energy and motivation. Another great advantage was that we got plenty of time to get to know each other: the project lasted almost a year. Not simply the fact that we did things together, but especially the way we did them, had a relational component, which motivated our increasing agency to accomplish something good and agreeable together.

*Jerry:* In smaller groups (4 students), I recall participation in two experiments in experimental psychology, with one professor coaching us, and we were to produce a joint paper on the basis of our results. Five years later the professor published a journal article, in part based on our results, and we were thanked in the footnote.[9] But of course, while this was collaboration between students, it was supervised, and our role was to do the dirty work, and to think along with the professor rather than create ideas. Of course, he was open for brilliant new ideas, but we simply lacked the knowledge. In the end, we knew what we had been told, and we knew each other better. Never seen these guys again.

*Jerry:* During the doctoral phase, a lot of workgroups again; we were learning in groups of 10–20, and sometimes I even participated in discussion. This was because I had started to know and like some of my fellow students, and discovered they were similar to me in many ways. I started discussing with them, not for the sake of learning, but because I liked being with them. Some of them raised my interest by discussing implications and alternatives to what we were taught, and even addressed my role in our discussions. It worked.

Development of collaborative relationships is likely to proceed slowly over a long period of time, and highly benefits from open-minded partcipants. Collaboration with people we do not feel much affinity with is possible, but preferably over a limited timescale, and with well-established procedures (such as carrying out a psychological experiment). Collaboration with people we like gives the greatest pleasure and may even bring about transformative learning.

*Michael:* University of Durham (UK), 1978: philosophy and psychology. Collaboration? Forget it: we were and were encouraged to be individuals, who each had to succeed, each be 'the best', future 'captains' (of industry, the army, the government, the university, etc.). Our only collaboration took place in the pub, discussing the courses we'd followed, over a few beers. That's collaboration, I suppose, sharing what you think, inventing stupid nicknames for the professors, sharing a laugh. But we never actually worked together, we were never asked to. In fact, no: not everyone really tried to be 'the best'. There were also some gentleman/gentlewoman loafers. They just wanted to get by, not get thrown out, do some theatre, rowing, perhaps meet a future spouse from their own social milieu. One very nice girl, an ambassador's daughter, came to see me one week before the final exams (I had never spoken to her before, although she was in my tutorial groups), to ask for advice, the key to passing the exam without really knowing anything. I cooperated, in telling her the right things to write in the exams, about Wittgenstein. She passed (only just).

It was an English professor who recently told me [JA] that collaboration was nonsense. Academic life was about bringing out the best in individuals. The individualistic tradition is *not* about differences between the owners and the workers; it is about becoming the best person you possibly can. This is a Protestant Christian idea and value: it is a sin to not develop to the full the 'talents' that God gave you. In this process, the professors are the masters, and full development of your talent requires them setting the highest standards for you to meet, thereby deliberately creating frustration for you to overcome. Incidentally, becoming smarter might allow you to become more important.

In this individualistic tradition, those who own the knowledge are the powerful ones; they form the academic aristocracy. From the side of the students, however, parasitic behaviour is accepted, as it is the result that counts, not the way to get there. This is competition, not collaboration, with a few winners and many losers.

*Jerry:* My final year before graduation was spent at another university, in Geneva, where I witnessed how a research group worked. It was a situation that I found out to be typical for research groups, a small room, many individuals, and occasional meetings during which one or two researchers presented their work and discussed it with others. Sometimes there were joint studies and joint publications. Within this group, and perhaps the situation of all participants working in the same room, it seemed to me that they all were quite aware of each other's work. I learned some French, and about how researchers interact and gossip. The level of discussion was far beyond my grasp of the domain and the French language. Reading their publications was the best I could do.

Academic contexts are examples of contexts with strong norms and rules. The challenge for newcomers is to become part of the academic group by mastering the required norms in appropriate behaviour. Without appropriation of the group norms and no record of excellence, participation is denied. In contrast, collaboration between equals, involved in an open inquiry process, can be quite productive. The same applies to informal collaboration, for the same reasons.

Some academic contexts are strongly anti-collaborative, whilst others are more open and receptive. Some traditions focus on the competitive game of achieving individual excellence. But for the system to survive, some collaboration seems to be essential. On the one hand, there is the strong desire to become part of some particular group. When ambition rises (this can be endless in academics), the desire for being part of specific groups develops. On the other hand, on the side of existing contexts of practice, collaboration starts with openness to participation of 'newbies', showing them how things work. This is the participation model of learning.[10] Is that collaborative, even sometimes, or should it be?

## 4   PhD and Beyond

*Michael:* My PhD. There again, no real 'working together'. But, we, the PhD students and the revered elders, the post-docs, were some kind of community. We had to be: the supervisors, professors, were always doing something else, or else going to London, Amsterdam,

Cal-i-forn-i-a. Or discussing with some other student who seemed to have greater needs for help (that was what they said). You started as something like a ship's cabin boy (or cat) and worked your way up to being a ship's mate, who could advise the new ones starting. I knew that if I couldn't see how to get that LISP or PROLOG program to work, or to format that bibliography, I could go and see Claire or Rick, or Mike; they'd come and help fix that function, with an avuncular smile, and joke about it in the pub later. All good fun. In particular, it was the women post-docs, surrogate elder sisters (Claire, Fiona, Sarah), who helped me most, with general life and PhD blues. I am eternally grateful to them, for good companionship and friendship.

So, no collaboration so far: that was somehow a balance between total individualism – 'MY PhD, MY original work' – and becoming part of a community, helping each other (at least some of us). But there was no real 'working together': each of us did our own PhD, or own research, and talked to the others about it. There were differences between people, in terms of how helpful they were willing to be. I don't think I was better at that, or worse, than anyone else. I do remember having helped the man in the office next to me ... he would appear, from time to time, in my doorway. "Errm, Michael", he would say; screwing up his face, "about Wittgenstein ...". Then he would ramble and struggle on in an incoherent way. But it didn't matter: I listened, as he struggled with himself. "So, what do you think is the answer?", he would usually end. I could sense that nothing I could say to him would be able to penetrate his personal struggle with coherence and understanding. "How about if we went to the common room and had a cup of tea?", I would say. By then, he would usually have found some kind of peace. That was the only way I thought I could help him. Not much; just being there, willing to listen. Drink tea. Smile a bit, and say "errmm" at more or less the right moments.

*Jerry:* My PhD work I recall as being lonely work. I was part of a research and teaching group, and everyone was busy with either their own teaching or their own research (mostly with teaching, it seemed), or participating in departmental meetings. I also had to spend two days a week on teaching. Compared to the situation for PhD researchers at universities now, thirty years later, it was paradise. But, in my experience, people were busy and did not have time for deep discussion with others. My supervisors did not apply their expertise in order to properly coach my research, in part because

I had taken a very experimental approach, and we had no deep discussions. Once I had an appointment with one of my supervisors and found the text I had worked on for a very long time in his trash bin. I did not take him seriously after that. The other supervisor mainly changed my (few) spelling errors and looked at my APA (American Psychological Association) standardised formatting of the text and references to the research literature. This was the first stage of word processors becoming available. There seemed to be no other PhDs to discuss with in the department. I got along best with a guy who later became a (successful) poet. He liked me and we both shared the feeling of alienation in an environment that looked a community but was deeply divided beneath the surface. I had to stumble for a while before I found people in the European context who worked on similar topics. After I had found them, finishing my PhD was much facilitated.

Without a proper community to be a part of, such as colleagues in the local context, or people involved in the same topic in various contexts, individual tasks involving deep knowledge are very very difficult to carry out. Collaboration can have the shape of sharing worries and issues, or jointly figuring out a solution for some predicament, but its main objective is learning to participate in the community one desires to be part of.

*Jerry:* A good example of collaborative teaching I experienced during my first years as an assistant. In the eighties, teachers at the department used to work in teams. No one told them to, they just did it. Especially with new topics this was a very productive situation. At some point I was asked to create a new course, about Intelligent Tutoring Systems. I knew something about some systems and was familiar with the mind-machine metaphor and computational techniques, but I knew two colleagues who were also interested in the same things, and probably knew things I did not know much about. The three of us, and later two of us, created the new course together, and, most importantly, did our teaching together. I remember great mutual support between us teachers, and actual learning, even with increasingly smaller numbers of students. Some of my weaknesses and lapses of attention were actively compensated by my colleagues. We did not really give each other much feedback or criticism (although they addressed my deadly tendency to end my teaching with the comment: "it does not really matter anyway"), but there was real collaboration. In a later stage of by career, I collaborated with another colleague on a 'Learning with New Media' course. Although we probably did not agree on many aspects of teaching and learning, we got along fine, and efficiently distributed the work according to our areas of interest. We did not need each other's feedback; our good personal relationship allowed us to give each other the room to do what we liked and were good at.

Collaboration in a team can mean compensating for each other's weaknesses, and combining each other's knowledge. In this sense a team is clearly better than an individual.

*Jerry:* How different was the course I had to organise with yet another colleague fifteen years later, who was so busy with his other duties, that he left organisation up to me. In a meeting he did his part and then either left the room or remained sitting behind his computer answering his email. I told him once I found this insulting, to hear he found my behaviour insulting too. After 27 years I left university, as I understood it to be definitively taken over by managers who were sensitive only to numbers. All the work was highly compartmentalised, individualised, and less and less determined by individual creativity and inspiration. Students (of course there were exceptions) seemed to have become only interested in making it through to the end rather than learning a thing or two.

Collaboration is a characteristic of a system. The aversion to collaboration is not only a bad sentiment; it can also be the wisdom to back out of a context that is not rewarding group performance, only individual excellence (or usability).

*Michael:* I think that my first experience of working in anything resembling a group, or a team, was after I finished my PhD. I went to France and worked in Lyon on a project financed by the European Union, about developing software that enabled people to make computer-based courses for industry. Of course, there was a local boss of the project: he wore a suit and tie, travelled a lot. I worked mostly with two other people I shared a big office with. We talked a lot across the top of our computers and had to write papers together. 'Together' usually meant we talked about what to write, then one person (usually me) wrote it, then the others read it and suggested changes to it.

I then got a permanent job in research. It's now a long story. The short version of that is that I worked in a team where there was the boss who expected us all to think the way she did, and to do what she said. I have never been good at being a slave, at least not where it involves thinking. I have worked on a farm, picking Brussels sprouts, where I had no problem in doing what the foreman said. But when it comes to thinking about things, research, I have my own ideas: I'm not able to think what other people want me to think. It just doesn't work that way.

Years passed. I gained my independence, my own small research team. Managers will say this is a mistake, but we were all friends, the five of us. We went out for pizza and beer often, after work, late into the evening. It's a mistake, managerially, of course: because if you become friends with your subordinates, you can't tell them off and tell them what to do. But I did not agree with telling anyone what to do and think: I thought it was about creating new ideas together, about collaboration, about everyone working on a problem because they were interested in it, passionately. That meant discussing together what to do. There were tensions, of course. I tried to sort them out. It was a lot of work. It was productive. We did together things none of us could have done alone, and I have good memories of that.

*Jerry:* Growing older, one gets the honour and pleasure of working with younger researchers, such as PhD students or post-docs. My supervision of these talented people was a mixed experience. I would have liked to collaborate on equal footing, but there always was this hierarchical difference, especially with male researchers. Without exception, they wanted power, refused to share results, and went for personal success, probably because they thought this was part of the system that I represented. With some female researchers (not with all) I developed better personal relationships, and, as a consequence, we had better scientific discussions, and they were more collaborative participants in our projects. With hindsight, I think they also felt a generation and power gap that I refused to recognise.

There is no single ideal form of collaboration: it depends on the task, the people, the system, the hierarchy. Writing together probably does not fit with the forward driving forces in writing; but the task lends itself very well to working together in several phases. Collaboration in a team can be much better than working alone or doing what the boss tells you: better results, deeper discussions, better relationships. It is hard to tell what comes first, maybe they all evolve together during collaboration.

*Michael:* I worked on quite a few EU-funded projects. That involved seeing a lot of other cities in Europe. A lot of airports, hotels, restaurants, meeting rooms. Mostly, we didn't collaborate. Because everyone had their own things at stake – career, boss on their backs, I don't know what – in their own institutions. It wasn't easy to understand what people in those central European countries had at stake. Quite a lot of walking around strange cities after restaurants. I did collaborate with the people in my own lab in France, and with a few friends in the project, I'd known before it started. But, we had each too much administrative work to do, to have the time to really collaborate. We did our own thing, then pieced it together at the end. And when we had done what was required, just sometimes, we could give ourselves the fun and pleasure of really creating something together, in a small group of people who had found each other in the project. It was good, sometimes: we invented things together we couldn't each have done alone.

*Michael:* I changed research teams a couple of times. Nowadays I collaborate with several other people, where I work, in Paris, and elsewhere in the world. What is in common about those collaborations? I think, mutual respect, for the ideas of the others, and for the other as a person. I have had a few bad experiences of collaboration: people who have tried to present my ideas as their own (every researcher has some such story). No problem: I now only work with people with respect to whom I know there is mutual respect and liking, on every level, ideas and the person. Academics are mostly egocentrics, who believe themselves to be (misunderstood) geniuses. They are required to be, since it takes a lot of dedication. So I decided, that, since they are all geniuses (including me, of course …) then I would choose to work with the geniuses with respect to whom there is genuine mutual respect, trust and shared interest.

*Jerry:* I liked working in an international context, on EU funded projects, where you would work with teams from various EU research institutes, all suffering from bureaucracy, lack of time and money, but often still inspired to share and extend ideas together. Here also, collaboration was far from ideal, people worked on their own thing, having interests of their own. But when thinking about new technology for supporting collaborative learning and actually having to build and test that technology, you cannot succeed without at least some collaboration. Therefore, the best collaboration probably develops in groups that do design and create. I liked the forward moving spirit of our projects, the interaction with some people that became friends, and others that remained indifferent. In my view, this could be the beginning stage of serious collaboration, but many circumstances prevented it from seriously developing, and it was restricted to incidental rather than being default mode of working together. Most colleagues take the default mode to be doing their own thing. I discovered I was less interested in individual stardom. What I was looking for was successful teamwork, and the activity itself being the main goal instead of some ambitious outcome.

It seems that collaboration is worth fighting for; and it often requires a fight to create free time and resources to be able to collaborate. It took a lot of experience before we realised that. Collaboration may fail with the wrong people, essentially when no trust is developed after a period of time. The academic world has an ambiguous rapport with collaboration, if not a negative one. We think that this precludes real progress.

As we have seen, simply putting people together for various reasons does not necessarily produce productive collaboration. We have provided many explanations for why this might be the case. However, seen from another perspective, can we say something about when the chances are high that collaboration will work, at least from the experiences we had, described in this chapter? It seems that collaboration works better when wise people who like and respect each other are grouped together, rather than eager and greedy ones. At this point, the foremost activities standing out as productive are those of creating something new whilst creating new rewarding working relationships. Working with minds not too different nor too similar, on a task that is not too easy, but within the reach of our imagination, jointly aiming for the creation of something which does not yet exist, openly and forward moving, not afraid to make mistakes, that is collaboration at its best. And probably what it has been made for.

Collaboration is crucial for the creation and design of new ideas. For this to work, we probably need teams of members with complementary expertise.

## 5    Main Ideas

There are different forms of collaboration, within different types of relationships contexts, rewards, outcomes and dynamics. In our lives, experiences with different forms of collaboration colours the meaning we give to the concept. In order to understand the concept 'collaboration' in a more scientific way, we need to carefully consider the roles of relationships, contexts, dynamics and outcomes.

We presented a short version of collaboration in our lives, in the form of a narrative, trying to preserve the colours and moods of the experience. Below, we list some of the main points that emerged.

We like to collaborate with friends, people with similar minds, people we trust, or with whom we develop a sense of trust over time.

It seems that joint objectives and respectfully engaging in joint activities are essential characteristics of collaboration. Obviously, there must be a contextual need for these, in order for collaboration to flourish.

Especially with children, collaboration can take on the form of role-play. This is like the individual pretend play with imagined roles that very young children engage in, now extended to real people and situations. This pretend play serves to increase our understanding of what others do, concerning what is possible and tolerated.[11]

Collaboration in music is important for sharing emotions and managing relational tension by increasing relational sensitivity and achieving mental balance.

Collaboration is at odds with hierarchy, power and external motivation. This makes it difficult to engage in collaboration in school contexts, where it is imposed upon the students by teachers.

Collaboration requires and hence develops the ability to explain oneself to others.

Differences in temperament, motivation, knowledge and skill between participants seem to increase tension, but can also be a productive source of learning and transformation. People have to (learn to) manage different sources of emotional tension in their collaboration.

Becoming a good collaborator in various contexts may take time to develop during childhood, adolescence and adulthood. It may require more explicit coaching during the adolescent years.

Collaboration may imply compensating for each other's weaknesses.

There is no single format for collaboration.

Collaboration seems fit the creation and design of new ideas. For this to work, we probably need teams of members with complementary expertise who find satisfaction also in getting to know each other.

### Notes

1  See Van Hoorn, Monighan-Nourot, Scales, and Alward (2014).

2   See Sawyer (2014).
3   See O'Dair (2014).
4   See Byrne (2012).
5   See Collins, Brown, and Newman (1987).
6   See Lesgold, Rubinson, Feltovich, Glaser, Klopfer, and Wang (1985).
7   See Illeris (2018).
8   See Watson (2010).
9   See ten Hoopen, Akerboom, and Raaymakers (1982).
10  See Sfard (1998).
11  See Wootton (2005).

## References

Byrne, D. (2012). *How music works*. San Francisco, CA: McSweeney's.

Collins, A., Brown, J. S., & Newman, S. E. (1987). *Cognitive apprenticeship: Teaching the craft of reading, writing and mathematics* (Technical report No. 403). Cambridge, MA: BBN Laboratories, Centre for the Study of Reading, University of Illinois.

Illeris, K. (2018). A comprehensive understanding of human learning. In *Contemporary theories of learning* (pp. 1–14). London: Routledge.

Lesgold, A., Rubinson, H., Feltovich, P., Glaser, R., Klopfer, D. D., & Wang, Y. (1985). Expertise in complex skills: Diagnosing X-ray pictures. In R. Glaser, M. Chi, & M. Farr (Eds.), *The nature of expertise* (pp. 311–342). Columbus, OH: National Center for Research in Vocational Education.

O'Dair, M. (2014). *Different every time: The authorised biography of Robert Wyatt*. London: Serpent's Tail.

Sawyer, R. K. (2014). *Group creativity: Music, theater, collaboration*. London: Psychology Press.

Sfard, A. (1998). On two metaphors for learning and the dangers of choosing just one. *Educational Researcher, 27*(2), 4–13.

ten Hoopen, G., Akerboom, S., & Raaymakers, E. (1982). Vibrotactual choice reaction time, tactile receptor systems and ideomotor compatibility. *Acta Psychologica, 50*(2), 143–157.

Van Hoorn, J. L., Monighan-Nourot, P., Scales, B., & Alward, K. R. (2014). *Play at the center of the curriculum*. London: Pearson.

Watson, P. (2010). *The German Genius: Europe's third renaissance, the second scientific revolution and the twentieth century*. City??: Harper/HarperCollins Publishers.

Wootton, A. J. (2005). *Interaction and the development of mind*. Cambridge: Cambridge University Press.

CHAPTER 3

# First Interlude

Let us return to our stories about doing things with our Dads. In Europe, those were probably the last days of the 'Dads' seen as figures of authority. And nowadays, since we are both Dads ourselves, we have different relationships with our children.

One major lesson seems to be that collaboration and authority do not mix well together. Neither does collaboration occur in systems where individual achievement is the dominant underlying ideology.

Things might have been different, with the Dads, in a way, if there could have been found – which was sometimes the case – things to do that both were genuinely interested in. That seems to be an important point: collaboration involves all genuinely being interested in doing the same thing.

FIGURE 3.1   Rembrandt painting: "The Anatomy Lesson of Dr. Nicolaes Tulp" (1632)
(https://upload.wikimedia.org/wikipedia/commons/4/4d/Rembrandt_-_The_Anatomy_Lesson_of_Dr_Nicolaes_Tulp.jpg)

Look at this painting by Rembrandt, in The Hague, where Jerry lives (Figure 3.1). In the painting, presumably all the men with hats are interested in the 'same thing': learning to dissect corpses. But they are all looking in different directions. What does that signify: no interest, no joint focus, no collaboration? They may be just standing there for a while, listening to what the teacher says, hopefully understanding what he means to convey. In fact, this painting of a group of persons was commissioned by each individual as a personal portrait.[1]

But perhaps let's not be *too* strict about what collaboration is, otherwise, probably almost nothing will fall under the definition. Collaboration seems to be a question of more-or-less. And in most things that people will do together, there will be parts on which they will collaborate, and others where they each do separate parts of the same output.

Look at the painting of Adam and Eve in the Garden of Eden, also in The Hague, in Figure 3.2. It was painted by two of the great geniuses of the day, Rubens and Brueghel. Weren't they in competition with each other? Probably yes. But in this case, they combined their skills to make a showpiece that was good for each of them. Apparently, according to the notice in the museum:

> although Brueghel was responsible for the composition, Rubens started the painting. Very sketchily, in thin paint, he painted Adam and Eve, the tree, the horse and the serpent. Then Brueghel took on the plants and animals, which he painted with encyclopædic precision in finishing paint.

FIGURE 3.2   The Garden of Eden with the Fall of Man or The Earthly Paradise with the Fall of Adam and Eve (1617) by Peter Paul Rubens and Jan Brueghel the Elder (https://commons.wikimedia.org/wiki/File:Jan_Brueghel_de_Oude_en_Peter_Paul_Rubens_-_Het_aards_paradijs_met_de_zondeval_van_Adam_en_Eva.jpg)

It looks like the two great masters collaborated on 'the idea of the painting'. Then they divided up the work, each doing what he did best (Rubens: naked human bodies; Brueghel: animals).

Figure 3.3 shows a much less artistic drawing, nowadays called a 'rich picture', showing one of our attempts to grapple with the complexity of collaboration during the writing of this book.

FIGURE 3.3    Mediating artefact (paper) of collaboration between Jerry and Michael on the nature of collaboration

The meaning of a particular collaborative activity is not collaboration itself, but meaning is to be found in what participants aim to achieve collaboratively. And a goal is meaningful within some context in which it is valued.

We are not saying that everything in life should be collaborative: we would still like to own and use, exclusively, our own toothbrushes. Rather, most important projects will involve parts, such as the overall design, where it's good to collaborate, and others where it's ok for each to do separate parts that can then be put together.

### Note

1   We thank Jay Lemke for pointing this out to us.

CHAPTER 4

# The Seven Samurai

We have written this book because we think that presenting collaboration in all its complexity, viewed from different sides and undertaken for different purposes, will lead an interested reader into reflection and greater understanding of collaboration. We think that lists of ideal characteristics of collaboration do not matter when one has to act in real life (see Chapter 11 of this book), and therefore one is better off acquiring a general feeling and understanding of situations of collaboration. As we will show in the chapters that follow, there are important differences between various instances of collaborative activity, depending on their goals and contexts. It is possible to collaborate on many tasks, but when is this collaboration for the better? And what does 'better' mean here? Better for whom? Is whether collaboration is 'better' than doing something alone in fact the point? Whether it is better or not, according to certain criteria, one could still choose to collaborate as a way of living one's life.

In this chapter we discuss the scenario of a Japanese 'western', taken from one of the best films ever, *Seven Samurai* (1954) by Akira Kurosawa. It is a work of fiction, loosely based on historical events. We will try to analyse collaboration between the stakeholders in the film, in relation to the complex purposes of the collaboration. Because it is a film, we are able to present a relatively complete picture of the actions, including emotions, collaborations, gestures, outcomes and consequences.

Reading this chapter will also provide the reader more insight into what we, as social scientists, tend to look for in interpreting collaborative activity.

We shall not attempt to summarise all of the film here, since readers could either see it, or else consult one of the many synopses available on the web. But very briefly, the film is set in 16th century Japan, during the 'warring states' period, and relates the story of a farming village that hires seven masterless samurai in order to prevent bandits from stealing their crops (again) once they have been harvested. Once a member of the village overhears the bandits' plan, the village elder is consulted: he advises to hire samurai – hungry ones, since the villagers have nothing to offer but their rice (in which case, they will be reduced to eating millet). Recruitment takes some time and involves many vicissitudes. But once six of the samurai arrive in the village, they are greeted with fear and mistrust. The seventh samurai is added to the group once he raises a false alarm, to make the villagers realise that they need more help. The samurai train the farmers, and fortifications are constructed. Their strategy is to gradually reduce the bandits' numbers by letting them into the village one by one, then killing each whilst preventing the others from entering. In the final battle, during a torrential downpour, the remaining bandits are allowed in, then killed, apart from their chief, who takes refuge in the village women's hut. At the price of personal mortal sacrifice, the chief is finally killed. The villagers return to tending their fields, and the remaining samurai reflect on the fact that it is the farmers who have won in the end.

*The Seven Samurai* is scripted for a long (more than 3 hours) film of intense emotional, partly collaborative, activities of two different groups of people. The joint motive of the two collaborating groups, farmers and samurai, is to beat a group of bandits and forever stop them from stealing the farmers' possessions, violating their women, and taking away their only source of income for a whole year: the products of their farmed lands. They agree on the preferred solution: killing all the bandits.

The samurai tell the villagers to prepare for the act of killing bandits by building fences and trenches around the village, to allow the bandits only one entrance, lure them in one by one, and kill them. The killing is done by a group of ten farmers poking the victim with their spears until he is dead. Samurai have the strategic roles of initial and additional killing and taking care of training the villagers, motivating them, and keeping watch all the time there is no attack, as well as monitoring the bandits, their attacks and their attempts to sneak into the village. The actual killing requires neither thinking nor collaboration: it is an individual act (even if ten farmers spear the same enemy at the same time). Engaging in the killing together certainly adds to this highly emotional experience.

The collaboration at *the micro-level* (the intersubjective level of actions and interactions, including emotions and thoughts) is present in well-synchronised building, training, watching, alerting, and fighting. Participants compensate and reinforce each other's strengths and weaknesses. The better they do this, the better their collaboration will be. At *the group level* (the community level capturing what a group does) there is the collaboration between the two groups, and the perception and experience of each other's actions and, especially, mistakes, including the development of improved mutual understanding and trust between groups. We may assume slow improvement at this level, but also some regression to previous states of collaboration. Collaboration itself is what develops here, and from our point of view, this is the most important development.

In addition to the individual level of learning and action, collaboration can be described both at the level of person-to-person interaction (interpersonal or intersubjective level) and at the level of the groups working together (community-level). The same phenomena can be described at both levels. The community level presumably has more impact on the intersubjective level than vice-versa and is more difficult to qualify on the basis of a single episode of interactions. It needs to be interpreted on the basis of changes in behaviour, especially inter-group interactions, over several episodes.

The collaboration between the farmers is difficult and very emotional. Their first joint deliberation is on the main square of the poor village. All sit down, or rather cower with their heads between their arms, not knowing how to deal with the threat of bandits showing up when their crop will be ready for harvesting. Sometimes a man or woman stands up and cries out in misery, amidst a strong collective display of fear and despair. We may have here a case of collaborative complaining: sharing emotions leading ultimately to shared action. Or at least shared relief.

A dialogue fragment from the beginning of *The Seven Samurai*:

1. *Woman (crying):* Taxes, war, forced labour, drought, and now the bandits. The Gods want us to die.
2. *Man (crying):* I'd rather die! (*Jumps forward, buries his head in the straw*)
3. *Man 2 (Manzō, sitting, grave voice):* Our rulers do nothing to protect us.
4. *Man 3 (stands up):* They should help us as well as tax us.
5. *Man 4 (nods in agreement):* The inspectors only come after a bandit raid.
6. *Woman 2 (stands up):* We'd do better to give our crops to the bandits and hang ourselves. Then our rulers would care about us (falls down crying).
7. *Man 5 (Rikichi, stands up):* Let's make bamboo spears. Kill all the bandits!
8. *Man 6 (Yohei, cries in fear):* You can't!
9. *Manzō:* That's impossible.
10. *Rikichi:* You kill samurai if you catch them; why not bandits? (*attacking Manzō*)
11. *Man 4 (keeping them apart):* This is no time for quarrelling.
12. *Manzō:* They'll kill us all if we lost, even pregnant women and babies.
13. *Rikichi:* Anything's better than this! Either we kill them, or they kill us!

THE SEVEN SAMURAI                                                                                  41

> 14. *Manzō:* We are born to suffer; it's our fate. (*Rikichi sits down, angry*) If they come, let's give them the crop without a struggle. But we'll ask them to spare us enough to live on. We'll beg them on our bended knees.
> 15. *Rikichi:* Do you think they'll listen? Remember what we endured to keep the little rice we have. (*Leaves the circle of men to cower*)

At the group level, the first six utterances, a joint activity, serve to share emotions by letting them flow, also to better understand and agree on the gravity of the situation, and to work towards the decision. From line 7 on, two men are having an argument, an interaction about what to do, producing pros and cons of two solutions: giving up or resisting. In a way, both exchanges are collaborative, but not all participants speak, only the most prominent ones. The sharing of emotions is collaborative because it is a joint way to express how the famers feel. Collaborative argumentation is a way to resolve a conflict politely, although many conflicts are not solved collaboratively at all. In this case, there are two men arguing for one of two extreme positions. They each generate a couple of reasons and carefully listen to what the other says, and this is a highly emotional experience. Argumentation can be collaborative in spite of the great emotional tension. It is a sign of consideration, exercised by volatile listening to what the other has to say, even though both parties try to convince each other, or rather: the group.

Sharing of emotions can be a collaborative activity at the group level. Argumentation can be collaborative as well (see Chapter 8 of this book), at the level of the two parties seriously considering each other's ideas, especially in times of crisis.

The villagers then decide to let the wisest man speak, and he orders them to go and hire strong and hungry samurai to help them. He is a wise man, so he already has imagined all pros and cons that he did not hear, and simply decides without explanation. Even if some may not agree with the old man's decision, it is accepted, because everybody understands that there are two possible positions, and only one can be opted for.

Of course, this was a scripted activity, the whole scene lasting only a couple of minutes. It is probable that in real life this would be much longer, although the degree of necessary elaboration for some types of decisions may be less in groups with more similar participants. Indeed, what we see is a quick flow of meaning between the participants, each completely grasping what the previous speaker wants to convey. They are all part of the same situation and have shared hardship together. There are no misunderstandings; rather, there is a lot of shared understanding and compassion. This makes joint deliberation easier, including strong emotional display.

Knowing each other well and sharing understanding of the situation greatly facilitate the amount of emotional tension a collaborative group can handle, and therefore motivates collaboration and decision-making.

A party of three is sent out to find samurai for help. This does not mean that all farmers feel comfortable with the decision of the old man. Not all samurai are honourable, apparently; they violate women, and farmers have killed some samurai in the past. The farmers decide to hide their women, and Shino has her hair cut by her father to look like a man. Most girls are terrified, but only Shino has her hair cut off. These are the feelings with which the farmers wait for the samurai to come, and it explains the cold reception when they arrive. Here we see a disadvantage of the group being all too similar: their collective lack of trust is bad for collaboration on the intergroup level.

Without a minimal level of trust, collaboration will not happen. Causes of present distrust are often in the past and have to be addressed, preferably beforehand.

If shared understanding does not adequately match with the current situation, being part of a homogeneous team may be a disadvantage.

The samurai do not know each other well, except for Kambei and Shichirōji, who have fought together. It is however clear that they share a code of conduct and ethical standards. The two exceptions are Katsushirō, who is a newbie, and Kikuchiyo, who is a bit of a rough character. The latter identifies with the farmers, and understands their fears, even sleeps with them in the same stable. This is an important contribution to building the trust essential for collaboration between the two groups. The seven samurai possess different skills of battle, are different masters of their arms, are of different temper, and mean well with the farmers in different ways. Their initial activities when they have arrived in the village are carried out individually: this can be called teaching, each according to the skills of the samurai (planning fortifications, training the farmers in fighting, including tactics and characteristics of the enemy, supervising the building of the fortifications, socialising with the farmers). Katsushirō almost instantly locates the beautiful woman, Shino, dressed like a boy, and starts building a relationship with her. The samurai lead the activities with the farmers; the two groups do not collaborate on equal terms. What is allowed to one is not allowed to the other group, and vice versa. Trust in the samurai as meaning well is slowly building; the same applies to the samurai's understanding of the farmers' general situation.

Trust can be built up by interest in the other group and by joint activities. For the build-up of trust, a positive affective climate and a good result contribute greatly.

In a collaborating group, differences of skills and strength can be a strong point.

Mutual consideration is greatly facilitated by a shared ethical code of conduct.

After a long period of preparation and waiting, three bandit scouts are caught by three of the samurai; they kill two and take one for questioning. The farmers want to kill the bandit, and an old woman, who has lost her son, comes with a knife and is allowed to use it against the bandit, who is then speared by many farmers, to the disgust of the samurai. Collaboration between the two parties has failed here. Farmers are used to letting their emotions prevail; the samurai are usually in control of their emotions.

Differences in expression or restraint of emotions can be a threat to a starting collaboration. Mutual understanding may help to sustain collaboration.

The location of the bandits' base camp is then discovered. A party of two farmers (who know the countryside) and three samurai ride out to attack the enemy early in the morning and kill as many as possible. They find the camp while the bandits are asleep, set fire to some huts and shoot (with bow and arrow) the enemies coming out. To his surprise, one of the farmers (Rikichi) finds his wife, long ago captured by the bandits, coming out of a burning house, then returning into the house in shame when she recognises the attackers. Samurai Heihachi tries to pull Rikichi back, who wants to go after his wife. Heihachi is then killed by a shotgun. The attackers retreat and return home. There, they organise a first funeral, samurai standing and farmers kneeling.

Fighting does not tolerate deliberation and reflection. It must be practiced to the extent of near automation, or that of tacit communication. Interpretation of the situation, reacting to the unpredictable, relies on immediately knowing (tacit understanding of) what the others do and think, and what to do. Professional football may be one of the few current (we write this in 2019) collaborative activities where this has evolved to a relatively high degree.

The differences in control, experience, and a surprise event made collaboration in the raiding party quite difficult, especially when speed and accuracy were asked for. In order for farmers to think and act like samurai, at least to the extent necessary for fighting together, long dialogic sessions would have been required, in combination with extensive exercise. With hindsight, the time for such activity probably was sufficient, and some lectures were provided by the samurai. However, for the farmers to understand what the samurai expected them to do without being told, which would afford effective collaboration, the pedagogical approach of incidental lecturing was not sufficient. As it stands now, the farmers take orders and carry them out, and things risk going wrong if they don't understand.

Telling people what to do, and also lecturing them, are primitive approaches, that may seem practical for learners who do not appear to have enough time, or are considered too different in their understanding to fully comprehend. In the best cases, these approaches lead to people doing the right thing in the same situation, but not in a different one.

After the raid, the bandits retaliate immediately, but find the village enclosed by fences. Desperately they circle around the village, looking for a weak spot. One arrow from a samurai hits its mark. Tension rises and Kambei tells farmers to shout battle cries. He deliberately has left one weak spot for the enemy to enter, into a trap of course. Bandits set fire to the houses outside the fences, including that of the old wise man. They attack during the night, six of them are killed, the farmers gain confidence.

The plan works fine so far, and as long as everyone plays his part well, collaboration will succeed. The enemy is desperate; we should not forget that they act out of a need for food, not just for the sake of it. However individual members of the bandit team are treated like animals by their chief, who sees no problem in killing somebody who made a mistake. They have one big asset, or rather three: they have gunpowder rifles. The cool samurai Kyuzo manages to capture one of the guns. Driven by need for admiration Kikuchiyo leaves his post to go out and capture another gun, and after some complications he succeeds. However, he returns with the enemy on his heels, and is scorned by Kambei for leaving his post. In battle one does not engage in individual actions! Indeed, bandits immediately attack from two sides; some bandits get through and kill some farmers with bow and arrow, including Yohei, who stood watch for Kikuchiyo. Gorobei is killed by gunshots. Thirteen bandits are still left, while seven were killed. The final battle will come soon.

In collaboration there is potential conflict between individual and group goals.

In this case, going for individual glory and praise succeeds at the individual level, but fails at the group level, as it leads to further fights and probably some losses, including the life of another samurai. Some of these things may just as well turn out fine, however. Obviously, when lives are at stake, one should carefully estimate the risks, but potential gain of individual heroism is also very large. In collaborative relationships the solution is in discussion, probably argumentative. In time of war, this is not always possible. Nevertheless, individuals in the two groups become aware of many aspects of collaboration, including the need to discuss issues.

How collaboration evolves over time, and in what direction, can be investigated at the individual, interpersonal, and group (community) levels, leading to different descriptions and interpretations of interdependent developments. Many developments are instigated at the interpersonal level, as we observe many one-to-one interactions having great impact on the flow of events as well as on development of collaboration. In scientific literature these three planes of development have been characterised as apprenticeship, guided participation and community processes. In a later chapter (Chapter 7), we will return to the development of collaboration.

For the development of collaboration, given where the two groups come from and what motivates their collaboration, we think that the level of interpersonal development is crucial. Barbara Rogoff[1] writes:

> The concept of *guided participation* refers to the processes and systems of involvement between people as they communicate and coordinate efforts while participating in culturally valued activity. This includes not only the face-to-face interaction ... but also the side-by-side joint participation that is frequent in everyday life and the more distal arrangements of people's activities that do not require co-presence (e.g., choices of where and with whom and with what materials and activities a person is involved). The 'guidance' referred to in guided participation involves the direction offered by cultural and social values, as well as social partners; the 'participation' in guided participation refers to observation, as well as hands-on involvement in an activity.

The group or community level involves taking up and gradually understanding (and also appropriating) how the community sees the world and why people behave as they do. It is better described by looking at the activities taken up after some discussion: how well are they executed, and to what extent is tacit understanding between participants already established?

Like any social activity, collaboration develops over time on three planes: the individual, the inter-personal, and the group-level. For our samurai-case, inter-group collaboration could be added to as a fourth level. Development at that level may also be (partly) grasped as guided participation, guided by the traditions and instruments at the disposal of the samurai, and knowledge of the topography and their shared understanding from the side of the villagers, whilst jointly participating in preparatory and actual activities involving the chasing of the bandits.

The final battle takes place on the next morning, rain pouring from the sky. The remaining bandits storm through the entrance and are attacked by the farmers and samurai. Chaos and nervousness rule. The bandit chief with his rifle manages to hide in the women's quarter and kills Kyuzo. Kikuchiyo storms at the chief, is hit, kills the chief with his sword, and then dies. It is over. And collaboration is over. The next scene shows singing farmers working on their fields, and the samurai that are left agree that the farmers are the winners. The samurai lost four men. The result of the collaboration is that the main objective has been achieved. All interaction between the two groups has stopped and the samurai leave the village. Societal norms preclude further bonding. All previous build-up of trust will be kept.

Taken as the activity of fighting the bandits, the collaboration was a great success. On the plane of fighting, both groups were compensating for each other's weaknesses: the small number of samurai, and the limited fighting skills of the farmers. The farmers have learned something about how samurai go about these matters. They may also have learned something about compassion, friendship, and consideration. They still think samurai are a little strange and can be dangerous too; but they have also seen their strong code of honour and resilience until death. They can distinguish the qualities of a good samurai.

The lost romantic souls of the surviving samurai have some added scars. They may have grasped the misery of the farmers, and maybe even the desperation of the bandits. They have understood more about why farmers act as they do, and to some extent, how to handle that. They may have understood something about the importance of trust and the role of emotions and fear. All of this is meaningful, coming from collaboration.

At the end of the film, two samurai witnessing singing farmers in the field suggest that we have an example of a missed opportunity: farmers failing to see the way of the samurai as meaningful for their own lives, or at least recognising the value of having collaborated with them. There seems not to have been any expansion of the farmers' horizons. This is a pity, but probably characteristic of normal life. For some reason, especially after highly emotional events, wars in particular, people want to return to their previous state of being as soon as possible. This means that the expansive learning[2] that might have been possible is not an automatic consequence of taking part in emotional and meaningful events. The most important outcomes (community level) of collaboration need reflection and moderation, the internal dynamics of their system need to be addressed and opened for change. Also, it seems clear that a challenge for change must be present: finding a new way of working in order to prevent some of the same issues from turning up again. It is clear the farmers do not define the issue as such, at least not at present. The real challenge for collaborative learning is the understanding of changing current practices (individual ways of working) to more collaborative forms.

It looks as if, in the seven samurai film, collaboration has not resulted in changes in the farmers' view or ways of working. For such changes to take place, a better understanding of the needs and the role of the system by its participants would be needed.

What can we learn about collaboration, from the film *The Seven Samurai*?

Emotions can hamper collaboration, but they can also help people to express themselves, as a basis for dissipating emotions and achieving better mutual understanding. Being able to handle strong emotions from others during collaboration probably requires knowing them well.

Shared codes of conduct and ethical principles greatly facilitate working together, as these shared aspects of behaviour allow for quick understanding and similar directions of thinking and acting.

Two different – and in a way opposed – community-based forms of collaboration are either grounded on complete openness and equality, or on clearly defined roles and scenarios. One could develop either form, but the underlying skills will be different. In this film we see an example of collaboration between very unequal teams. If there is no time for bridging inequality, for example by dialogic activities, it seems that clear instruction of roles and tasks are crucial. However, this risks problems when something unexpected happens.

In the end, it is the overarching, societal or systemic rules and norms that determine the nature and consequences of collaboration. Without any systemic support, attitudes and motivations to collaborate will not change easily, because they are part of that same system. The collaboration described here was a bottom-up violation of the rules, turning out positively in the end.

Acting together for some purpose does not inevitably result in (shared) understanding of what happened and why, even in the case of success. This is not strange at all; it has been found for individual activities as well.[3] A shared experience does not automatically entail shared learning. Developing a shared view requires openness towards developing one, and deliberate attention and reflection on what is happening. Only when there is ample time and openness for endless deliberation and reflection, we may learn how to advance as a group.

### Notes

1   See Rogoff (2008).
2   See Engeström (2014).
3   See Van Amelsvoort, Andriessen, and Kanselaar (2007) and Bereiter (1995).

## References

Bereiter, C. (1995). A dispositional view of transfer. In A. Marini & R. Genereux (Eds.), *Teaching for transfer: Fostering generalization in learning* (pp. 21–34). Mahwah, NJ: Lawrence Erlbaum Associates.

Engeström, Y. (2014). *Learning by expanding*. Cambridge: Cambridge University Press.

Rogoff, B. (2008). Observing sociocultural activity on three planes: Participatory appropriation, guided participation, and apprenticeship. *Pedagogy and Practice: Culture and Identities*, 58–74.

Van Amelsvoort, M., Andriessen, J., & Kanselaar, G. (2007). Representational tools in computer-supported collaborative argumentation-based learning: How dyads work with constructed and inspected argumentative diagrams. *The Journal of the Learning Sciences, 16*(4), 485–521.

CHAPTER 5

# Spaces for Collaboration

The previous chapter can be taken as an illustration of a situation where collaboration was a vital necessity. This is not uniquely human, similar behaviour has been found in other primates.[1] In this case the farmers asked the samurai to help them within a cooperation for mutual benefit. Such benefit needs to be negotiated tactfully. When some agreement has been negotiated, we may still expect collaboration to develop slowly, in parallel with increasing self-awareness. Various types of ideas, feelings, and actions need to coalesce into something more integrated. To what extent can such developments be supported and predicted? In this chapter we briefly look at the role of context, situations and spaces in the emergence of collaboration.

FIGURE 5.1   Scene from the Seven Samurai: Samurai Kikuchiyo with the poor farmers

In the samurai story of the previous chapter, there were two very unequal teams collaborating for the benefit of one team, the farmers. Through their goal-directed activities, as well as their discussions, farmers and samurai had interactions in which emotions were prominent, especially those of the farmers. In the picture of Figure 5.1, we see Kikuchiyo, a rough samurai, who understands the farmers quite well, and is quite disgusted with their attitudes, especially their previous killing of samurai. For the sake of their collaboration, he discusses with the farmers and tries to convince them what to do, and to trust the current group of samurai. What developed over time as a consequence of such interactions was better understanding of the situation of the farmers by the samurai. This learning was mediated through the emotions of the farmers, depicted in the film (and on the picture) as simple men, who by expressing their feelings, showed what they thought was good or bad, difficult or important, etc. In other words, through their emotions they expressed the meanings they attributed to the things in their world. If emotions were left out of the equation, understanding meaning-making in collaboration will be limited. The samurai story can be taken as an example of how people *appropriate a situation* in which they understand the need to collaborate, and they do this by overtly expressing emotions rather than rational thoughts.

Ideally speaking, people appropriate a collaborative situation as follows: they try and make sense of what the situation is, why it is what it is, how to behave to achieve some goals, what concepts are important, or more basically, what the characteristic objects and rituals are. In their attempts to accommodate to the situation, people make the situation their own. Not concepts, but situations are the units of collaborative learning. Situations afford meaning making: the tangible object is already there, but the participants must collaborate to evolve towards a shared view of it, as in seeing things from the same angle.[2]

Appropriation is not a smooth process, the reflection on situations may not be as smooth, or may even be absent; people may simply act and see what happens. Collaboration in the real world rarely develops from scratch: often individuals join already existing groups with already established collaborative cultures. It is quite normal that new people are introduced into already existing communities whose participants collaborate for mutual benefit. Often such inaugurations happen in particular physical contexts. In the novel *World Shadow* by Nir Baram[3] we can read the story of a character, a young man, son of a father who developed his own profession: writing dying people's autobiographies. Especially in the world of the rich, there was sufficient demand for this craft, and it gave the father access to a network of international businessmen. The father despised the rich and powerful, although he worked for them, but he did not mind his son being introduced into such a network, when this son was asked by an influential American director of a large financial organisation to create a start-up in Israel. This starting-up organisation would not be directly about making money but rather about supporting underprivileged groups in some way. The details of this do not matter for our purpose; what is interesting here are the rich and presumably accurate descriptions of how the powerful make money through collaboration. The starting organisation was a cover up to participate in the collaborative network of the powerful.

The group of powerful people, to which our hero is being introduced, consists of businessman, but also academics from university, politicians, artists and others who meet every week in some restaurant to discuss the opportunities that emerge during the nineties, the era of peace and globalisation, at least in the promised land.

This kind of meeting reminds us of how people used to share new information in the days when there were no newspapers, and no last-minute information available from other media. In 1760, people used to meet in large coffee houses where the latest novelties were exchanged and discussed. They were seated on long benches behind large tables, speaking loudly about the news, listening to newcomers and what they had to say, drinking alcohol and discussing interpretations. For the more sophisticated, there were particular coffee houses, as in the painting from a Vienna Coffeehouse in 1900 (see Figure 5.2). Literary, political and philosophical groups called salons were held in private houses.

FIGURE 5.2  "Zu den blauen Flaschen", Vienna Coffeehouse around 1900 (https://commons.wikimedia.org/wiki/File:Zu_den_blauen_Flaschen_painting_c1900.jpg)

In Baram's novel, similar interactions as in the old coffee houses take place between influential people in late 20th century Jerusalem. What we have here is a somewhat ritualistic form of collaboration with a number of remarkable features. Although participants seem similar, they are not: there is a hierarchy within the group, and some have more power than others. The later in the evening it gets, the more important the discussion becomes, but also less transparent. Although information is shared, not all of it is; and the same applies to opinions, political stances, or personal information. Everybody gets a chance to speak, but you will be accepted only if your talk is interesting and contributes to creating new ideas and opportunities for others in the group. If your contribution is not interesting you are supposed to shut up and eventually disappear, without being told. On the other hand, all new opportunities mentioned by anyone in the group will be actively considered. New names are often invited to the restaurant, or meeting them can be the goal of some journey abroad. In this way, the network is extended with new business opportunities. Some of these opportunities involve arms and warfare, in spite of the idealistic nature of the people in the network: their stated goals are innovation and progress.

Seen from the viewpoint of potential collaboration, this type of interaction results in the efficient formation of extended networks. In a way, people are pawns in each other's games, and these games are often not collaborative at all. The purpose of the collaborative network is to inform each other about all opportunities and to share them with other members, if deemed useful or out of courtesy because of some favour owed. The evenings serve to effectively share the latest developments, discuss opportunities and to find partners for new enterprises. In order to be successful, one needs to be part of the network, whose function is not collaboration, but to be a *structure* from which collaboration may fruitfully evolve. Collaborations start when some network members decide to undertake *action* together.

Such structures have always existed and may be the main vehicle for the powerful to stay in position or to extend their power. Newcomers are invited by co-optation, and it matters by whom the newcomer is introduced. Newcomers should quickly learn the codes of conduct, to move from the periphery to the centre, and it obviously helps when the newcomer is from a family familiar with the rules. What helps most, however, is when the newcomer is influential, knows a lot of powerful people, and is willing to exploit this influence to the benefit of members of the network, especially in newly to be explored cultures.

What powerful people understand is that their world turns around doing each other favours. These favours can be small, like buying someone a new suit from a famous store in Munich, where you happen to be traveling to. Sometimes people do not understand what the favour is good for. Sometimes people do not understand why a certain activity is beneficial for someone else. When newcomers get more deeply involved in the network, this does not lead to more clarity about real motives and sympathies, nor about the processes that are going on behind the scenes. This sounds similar to what some of us experience as scientists: the more we seem to know about some phenomena, the less we are able to understand them, and the more difficult it becomes to explain them to less specialised people.

Two points need to be drawn out from this chapter. One is that collaborative situations always have structure. This structure is the physical space for collaboration, including the rules, norms and scaffolds that have evolved over time. Collaboration is always influenced by the situational structure in which it takes place. If you want to understand collaboration, look at the structure.

The second conclusion is the opposite: structure is dynamic, and should allow deviations and errors, at least to some degree. While the term structure suggests something consistent, it needs to be flexible enough to meet new challenges and objectives, such as fighting the bandits instead of meeting their demands. There always is a tension between structure and the actions it allows.[4]

To conclude this chapter, it is interesting to reflect on the types of physical spaces that have been designed for collaboration. We discussed some examples above, including London coffee houses.

Figure 5.3 shows a new type of 'space', or cubicle, that has been designed for periodic collaboration, in a general office environment that is otherwise designed for individuals to work at their own desks.

FIGURE 5.3   A new office space for collaboration (drawing by Roxane Oudart-Détienne)

We can contrast this cubicle with the small space in which the authors collaborated on finalising the manuscript for this book, in summer 2019 (see Figure 5.4). It is a traditional bar in a tourist town in Yorkshire.

Why would we prefer this type of space to the space shown in Figure 5.3? After all, the Yorkshire bar was noisy and we were forced, against our will, to buy drinks periodically, in order to justify our presence. Of course, we were free to stand up, walk around, sit back down or simply leave and continue somewhere else. That does not seem to be the case with the futuristic 'pod' for collaboration shown above. Frankly, to us it appears false, antiseptic, a place that would stifle group creativity. Which leads us to the following question: is there not something strange, or even contradictory, with the idea of someone or some institution telling you that "you will collaborate, here, now, right there!" (recall the example in Chapter 1 of teachers telling students to collaborate). Doesn't collaboration presuppose a different, more free, mode of life? A life in which people do their work, but move freely around, deciding when and where they will collaborate with others.

FIGURE 5.4    The authors' collaboration space in summer 2019

## Notes

1  See De Waal (2010).
2  See Bergson (1896/2012).
3  See Baram (2015).
4  See Giddens (1986).

## References

Baram, N. (2015). *World shadow*. Amsterdam: De Bezige Bij.

Bergson, H. (2012). *Matière et mémoire: essai sur la relation du corps à l'esprit*. Paris, France: Flammarion. (Original work published 1896)

De Waal, F. (2010). *The age of empathy: Nature's lessons for a kinder society*. New York, NY: Broadway Books.

Giddens, A. (1986). *The constitution of society: Outline of the theory of structuration* (Vol. 349). Oakland, CA: University of California Press.

CHAPTER 6

# Second Interlude

So far, we have explored many different facets of the warp and weft of collaboration by giving many examples of how genuine collaboration can arise, over spaces and times. Collaboration is in fact more prevalent than we may have suggested. Here are three types of situations where collaboration often occurs:

1. *Game situations*, in which different roles can be acted out in concertation, needing resolution of lifelike dilemmas, or made-up predicaments. In Chapter 2, we discussed some such examples of children's play, where collaboration happens within some type of framework, including rules, obvious actions and examples. In addition, there are the motivating and capturing elements that will keep participants going.
2. *Life threatening situations*, in which it is found that working together is the only way out. Of course, this is the case of the seven samurai discussed earlier. A situation being life threatening is not sufficient for collaboration to occur; but when the participants (or some of them) realise that collaboration is an option, it may turn out to be very beneficial for them.
3. *Open, creative situations*, involving equal minds, sharing joint purposes, agency, willingness to learn and to understand. We have seen several kinds of professionals joining together, in places where food and drink is served.

In this short interlude we would like to reflect a little further on each of these cases.

What about games? In terms of collaboration, we conjecture that the emergence of games, involving a limited number of rules, roles, and activities – such as hide and seek, marbles, mommies and daddies, chess – stems from the simple motivation of being together, which is achieved by doing something together. This behaviour might be typically human (or primate), i.e. bonding for the sake of being together.[1]

Of course, competing and winning can be fun. But the *collaborative experience* is a special type of emotion; a game is shared fun (for all) to the extent that it is collaborative.

Some competitive games can be very collaborative, as long as winning or losing does not have to lead to shame or disgrace. Many kids understand this and are able to support the loser, or to adapt the rules, so that everyone has an equal chance. Competition and collaboration are not necessarily opposing each other in these circumstances (Figure 6.1).

FIGURE 6.1   Fun in family board game (drawing by Roxane Oudart-Détienne)

With older kids, and even for adults, games can be more complicated and the rules may lead their own lives; games can become addictive or specialised. At such levels of development of the activity, collaboration is no longer a primary goal. Games may require high skills, which are beyond the scope of just anyone, but may still attract many players and spectators.

The collaborative activity itself during games can be crucial. Football teams need to fine-tune their collaboration in order to win, although there seems to be ample room for individual excellence (Figure 6.2). These individuals can only excel because there is a team backing them up.[2]

Many rules and regulations, favouring some type of outcome or process may be invented to streamline the game processes. These rules may become dominant and constrain collaboration, which changes its original motivation, which was playing together. At some point such regulation may resemble a situation that, in education, is called 'scripting' of individual or group activities, in which they proceed according to a very strict framework, in time, with the aim (of the designers of the situation) of leading to very specific (learning) goals.[3] A collaborative script is a *contradictio in terminis*, like 'planned spontaneity'.[4]

FIGURE 6.2
Spectators before a football match (Bradford City versus Plymouth, November 2017)

What about life-threatening situations? Of course, they are a special case, in which participants can only be saved from some predicament by acting together, often in very specific ways. We have discussed the seven samurai. Other well know examples include groups of people cast away on desert islands, sports teams surviving by anthropophagy in the Andes after a plane-crash, someone being attacked in public when intervention is needed, a poorly playing football team facing defeat, people hiding persecuted Jews behind a secret door in their house during WW2, etc. Extreme situations can bring out the best or the worst in people. Collaboration comes to life because of the lives being threatened, and disappears immediately after this is longer the case. Many animals stay together during danger, to lessen the impact of an enemy attack, or to be able to defend the group. *Collaboration is preservation of the group*; the group is primary. This idea corresponds more to Japanese culture – the concept of *Wa*, or group harmony – than to European and American capitalistic and individualistic competition.

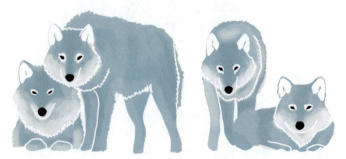

FIGURE 6.3    The wolf pack, protecting itself (drawing by Roxane Oudart-Détienne)

FIGURE 6.4  Collaboration in an extreme situation: old farmer lady checking out a Samurai, and vice versa

Collaboration in response to extreme conditions, with the aim of preserving the group, demands co-creating joint meaning of how to deal with the predicament and what the group is in the first place (Figure 6.4). Such collaboration may also be required in more mundane situations, such as for example when small groups are under time pressure, or have to make practical arrangements when expected solutions are not available (e.g. the restaurant is closed, the mountain hut is locked, etc.). It is not hard to imagine some individuals in such situations retreating from the group.

Now for the most general situation – the open situation, creative minds meeting.

Vera John-Steiner[5] describes many such collaborations, often between gifted individuals over their lifetimes, producing ground-breaking discoveries, such as in the cases of Jean-Paul Sartre and Simone de Beauvoir, Henry Miller and Anaïs Nin, Marie and Pierre Curie(-Skłodowska), Martha Graham and Erick Hawkins, and Georgia O'Keeffe and Alfred Stieglitz; the productive partnerships of Pablo Picasso and Georges Braque, Albert Einstein and Marcel Grossman, Aaron Copland and Leonard Bernstein, and Freeman Dyson and Richard Feynman; the familial collaborations of Thomas and Heinrich Mann, Hubert and Stuart Dreyfus, and Margaret Mead, Gregory Bateson and Mary Catherine Bateson; and the larger ensembles of The Guarneri String Quartet, Lee Strasburg, Harold Clurman and The Group Theatre, and such feminist groups as The Stone Center and the authors of Women's Ways of Knowing. Many of these collaborators complemented each other, meshing different backgrounds and forms into fresh styles, while others completely transformed their fields.

R. Keith Sawyer's book *Group Genius*[6] proposes that creativity is always collaborative, even when you are alone. Sharing the results of the author's own research on jazz groups, theatre ensembles, and conversation analysis, the book shows us how to be more creative in collaborative group settings, how to change organisational dynamics for the better, and how to tap into our own reserves of creativity. Collaborative creativity has become a very popular theme, thanks to this book.

It looks as if the world is full of examples of collaboration, including its creative variety. However, if we were to look in detail into each of these cases of collaborative genius, in the light of the basic characteristics of collaboration that we have discussed so far, this might raise questions as to just how collaborative these cases are. We leave such an examination to the care of the interested reader .... One could have various more or less strict visions of what collaboration is; and one could ask how useful it would be to explore them, in order to come up with so-called definitive answers. And yet, ... whose point of view is the point of view from nowhere? Who is to say and to analyse? – the participants themselves, researchers, observers? We rest our case at this point, in this brief – and optimistic, with respect to collaboration – interlude.

We have been considering collaboration in the wild: it is or can be everywhere. It can arise from everyday life, from play, dramatic circumstances and enriching creativity, and in so doing re-affirm, preserve the group, which remains once the circumstances change and collaboration dissipates. Collaboration strengthens interpersonal bonds, personal and interpersonal awareness.

### Notes

1 See Crook (2013).
2 "I was guarding Paul and sagging off him to help my teammates play defense. Our opponents collectively realized that I was leaving Paul to double-team whoever had the ball, so our foes began passing the ball to Paul. He caught the ball and scored a couple of shots. I adjusted by sticking close to Paul, but by then his teammates had realized that he was 'hot,' so they began to pick and pass. They set picks by getting in my way, freeing Paul. Then, they would pass him the ball and he would score again. My teammates grasped what Paul and his teammates were doing to me, so they began to help me guard Paul" (from Sawyer, 2015, p. 31).
3 See Weinberger, Ertl, Fischer, and Mandl (2005).
4 See Dillenbourg (2002).
5 See John-Steiner (2006).
6 See Sawyer (2007).

## References

Crook, C. K. (2013). Varieties of "togetherness" in learning – And their mediation. In M. J. Baker, J. Andriessen, & S. Jarvela (Eds.), *Affective learning together: Social and emotional dimensions of collaborative learning* (pp. 33–51). London: Routledge.

Dillenbourg, P. (2002). *Over-scripting CSCL: The risks of blending collaborative learning with instructional design.* Retrieved from https://telearn.archives-ouvertes.fr/hal-00190230/

John-Steiner, V. (2006). *Creative collaboration.* Oxford: Oxford University Press.

Sawyer, K. (2015). Group flow and group genius. *The NAMTA Journal, 40*(3), 29–51.

Sawyer, K. (2017). *Group genius: The creative power of collaboration.* New York, NY: Basic Books.

Weinberger, A., Ertl, B., Fischer, F., & Mandl, H. (2005). Epistemic and social scripts in computer-supported collaborative learning. *Instructional Science, 33*(1), 1–30. https://doi.org/10.1007/s11251-004-2322-4

CHAPTER 7

# Collaborating and Learning

At the end of the Samurai story (Chapter 4), we concluded that while there was collaboration between the farmers and the Samurai in fighting the bandits, both groups simply fell back into their old (and natural) ways of life. What could they taken away from all the turmoil? In other words, didn't they learn something? Although this was an example from a film, we can ask ourselves the question: how do we know about *any* learning taking place, and why *should* there be a change of views or ways of working as a result of collaborative activity? From all this effort and turmoil, we might expect some legacy. Wouldn't we expect the farmers to have improved their capacity for resisting the next gang of bandits? They now know where and how to build trenches and traps. And wouldn't we expect a relational legacy: what about farmers and samurai having gained in their understanding of *each other*, and not only in the context of fighting bandits together?

In this chapter, first, we suppose a relationship between the experience of collaboration and different outcomes of learning: changes in skills, strategies, relations, attitudes, etc. We learn from collaboration, and we learn to collaborate. On the other hand, this supposed relationship is rather vague: what is this learning precisely, and how does it relate to collaboration, what do we learn, and what not? Can such learning be predicted in some way, isn't there a way to support collaborative learning, and can collaboration be exploited in schools to support learning? These are the topics of the current chapter. It is no easy story.

Before dealing with these difficult questions, it must be realised that learning is an academic *concept* (an abstract entity), invented to make sense of some peculiar type of activity.[1] Collaboration is one too. Academic concepts are good for academics: they study the stretch and fabric of concepts. This does not imply that such concepts 'exist' as we define them, nor that they have constant and unequivocal meanings in everyone's experience. We need concepts, but they tend to suggest stability, whilst their meanings are evolving all the time. Of course, everyone, scientist or not, invents and uses concepts as well.[2] On the other hand, we do not focus particularly on the everyday meaning of the term 'learning' either: memory of facts or mastery of procedures, or anything else that is acquired through repetition, direct instruction and a lot of practice. For a long time, the study of learning was about individuals acquiring some type of knowledge in experimental conditions. For our interest in collaboration, we focus on the subjective experience[3] as well as on the actions associated with learning, rather than on abstract definitions or outcomes. We will try to provide some narrative to the rather academic text in this chapter.

## 1 A View on Learning

> A Samurai wanders along a sandy road in a small village. The inhabitants live in shacks made of clay and bamboo. It is quiet at this time of day. Our Samurai has never been in this village before, most of his life he has served a master, who owned a castle. Most of his duties were inside that castle. There, he spent his time perfecting his fighting skills, and also, he taught his skills in a small group of young men. They practised many hours each day. He could tell many stories about his pupils and how much they differed in the ways they tried to master the skill of sword fighting. But now he was in this little village, not really knowing what to do. So, he looked and smelled, and listened to the sounds. He heard some music coming out from a hut when he passed it. He stopped to listen to it for a while, but then the music stopped, probably because he was noticed. He understood that he was not trusted. Not yet. He decided that he should work on gaining the trust of the villagers, although he knew other Samurai would prefer to maintain distance.

Learning is always happening in our lives, even when we do not *deliberately* strive for it. We learn when we listen to the news, or enjoy listening to music; we are learning to fit in, or to stay away. Fundamentally, we learn how to act, or more precisely, what possible action to choose,[4] like finding our way home from work or addressing a teacher. Over time, we may acquire skills, such as fighting with a sword (in the case of Samurai), because we actively engaged in supervised training sessions. It could be that we have been told how to find our way home, but we may also have discovered ourselves, because our mother took us to school every day, acting as our guide.

The fundamental activity of humans in real world situations is called *meaning making*, or making sense of a situation, incorporating what is experienced.[5] The meanings we make provide us with the possibilities for further action.[6] Meaning making is not confined to facts or concepts, but involves the whole of experience, including related thoughts, feelings, motives, objects, and, crucially, other people.[7] This implies that the same event, experienced at different moments or by different people, can be interpreted in entirely different ways. The *narratives* we tell (or make up) of our experiences may capture such interpretation. Or, in Bruner's words, *ordinary people go about meaning making by telling stories*.

*We understand learning as making sense of the world through meaning making.* People do it all the time, assimilating and accommodating[8] their understanding of the world as they interact in various situations.[9] As a consequence, we can handle more complex and different situations because we can relate to more complex recollections, and better focus on what matters to us.

> To support the villagers with protecting themselves against the gang of thieves, the Samurai decided to teach these villagers how to defend themselves. The leader of the Samurai wanted to call all villagers to the town hall and explain to them what to do. He thought his explanations, combined with demonstrations by his fellow Samurai and practical exercises for the villagers, would be sufficient for them to understand the first principles of proper defence. Another Samurai, a former teacher of martial arts, thought that explanation was futile. Drilling them would do the trick. Drilling by frequent exercise and feedback would be the best way, he thought. Samurai number 1 was reluctant. He was convinced that explanations were crucial. How else would they be able to understand what they were supposed to do? A third Samurai suggested it would be a good idea to ask the villagers what they already knew. That would save some explanation time, and the training could start from there. Surely, the villagers had already acquired some way of defending themselves from previous experiences. Finally, they approached the villagers with the question of how they would like to be taught. One villager immediately said: let's fight between ourselves, with blunt weapons, but still a fight, with winners and losers, and prizes!

There seem to be 'types' of learning. A distinction often made in the research literature is between learning by *discovery* and learning by being *instructed*.[10]

*Instruction* aims at acquisition of specified knowledge (often by a student), as part of a designed curriculum (a series of instructions), guided by external agency (often a teacher). What instruction does is to direct a learner's focus, restricting what should be learned, at the same time socialising learners towards a focus on authority. This view of *education* corresponds to learning by being told.

*Discovery learning* is guided by the agency of the learner, who often acts as participant in a meaningful activity in a social context (i.e. a context in which we interact with other *people*) aiming for some shared objective. What *discovery* does is to leave it to the learners, allowing for mistakes, wrong tracks, and even dead ends, affording learning by enabling learners to embrace *agency*. Crucially, the experience of acting responsibly to achieve some objective is part of discovery learning, not of instruction. We think this is essential for development of agency in later life, when we cannot rely (but seem to do so, often by preference) on what some people tell us to do or to think.[11] The resources for learning within the two views (discovery *versus* instruction) are also different. In current educational systems, discovery has a minor role; there is a tendency for increased control by relentless testing,[12] and discovery is hard to control and test. However, in the real world, most learning is of the participatory, situational kind, relying more on discovery than on being told. As a consequence, school-learning remains only loosely related to the agency we may need to survive in the real world.[13]

The essential difference between types of learning relates to the types of activity they are meant for. We usually learn in the context of being engaged in some specific activity; therefore, many scientists claim that most learning is *situated*.[14] However, we have to realise that we also take much from previous activities: previous experience (or the meaning making derived from it) has great impact on how we learn and act here and now.[15] The term 'situated' learning stresses the fact that most learning takes place in context and should be understood within it. The social interaction that takes place between participants in a situation is crucial for such learning.[16] We think that the richness of an activity allows it to be connected to other recollections, of different types. This creates richer memories and more complex learning. The fundamental failure in education is in promoting the idea that children should learn that there are true concepts and true answers.

Our interest is in situations in which more people than the individual are involved – in other words, in *social or intersubjective learning*. Being engaged in some (social) activity does not necessarily imply that participants are always paying attention to what they are supposed to: they may focus on the nice looks of some women or men, instead of carefully focusing on what is being done. In addition, individual motivations for participation may differ. It makes sense to suppose that some participants in an interactive activity are not always *constructive*,[17] especially when the activity does not motivate them. In many situations, such as in a meeting room, not all participants will be trying to meaningfully contribute to the issue. This could be due to a lack of interest, but they can also be political motives. An example of the latter is when people block solutions by raising objections all the time, or not contributing at all. Such behaviour does not advance the issue, which may be the whole point of it. Some people have developed great expertise in raising objections; in other words, social learning can also mean learning to obstruct, or to inflict unproductive views.[18] Other participants, who do not fully understand the goals of such individuals, may learn the same behaviour and apply it to the wrong situations. The way we learn (or collaborate) can be explained by examining why and where we learn (or collaborate). Crucially, we learn by *being active* and what we learn depends on *why* we are active.

We propose that learning from social activities will be richer when participants collaborate. This is because collaboration, when seriously enacted, calls for active sharing and relating.

There are many scholars who insist on a more profound kind of learning, involving *reflection* or inspiration after the action. This kind of learning is based on good thinking: we do not take anything at its face value, but we ponder about some idea or concept, until some satisfactory state of belief or understanding has been achieved. This requires suspension of being satisfied with a current state of understanding, and the ability to live with the tension of not being entirely satisfied.[19] As we know, some people are easily satisfied; others are never satisfied. In the context of leisure, the first attitude is to be preferred; in the context of doing science, the latter attitude is much better. That is why science is difficult and cannot be expressed in simple terms. Prolonged reflection is sometimes called *deep learning*, or the learning contributing to intelligent action,[20] overriding actual experience.[21] Some may think deep learning only happens in isolated silence. We however support the contention that reflective thinking proceeds in a way that is akin to dialogue,[22] and that individual thinking can lead to erratic conclusions and further mistakes.[23]

FIGURE 7.1
The Thinker, Auguste Rodin (1903), symbolising reflection (https://pxhere.com/en/photo/668771)

> In addition to the villagers acquiring some basic fighting skills, the village itself also needed physical defence structures: walls, ditches, watch towers, quick transportation allies, schemes and locations for watching the village, many things that the Samurai preferred to set up themselves. Their leader tried to concoct a complete overview, but he failed. He discovered that the Samurai lacked essential knowledge about the village; they first needed to explore its strengths and weaknesses. It would be better to explore this in small teams, each team focussing on a specific aspect of defence. Villagers needed to participate in these explorations, since they knew their village best. The Samurai discovered that the villagers were expert in identifying the characteristics of the soil. This was very helpful in figuring out where to put the strategic defence structures.

Various ways of supporting learning have been proposed in the educational literature. Because, in our view, learning rests on our meaning making of a *situation*, only holistic structuring makes sense. This means creating or structuring situations (in education) in which relevant agency, reflection and progress are tangible affordances. Such a situation could include discussing a picture of someone's bedroom in kindergarten. Another situation could support constructing explanations for complex physical phenomena such as gravitational forces in secondary school. Because the situations are holistic, telling how events evolve, including the emotions, cognitions, relations and actions of the characters, we think that *narratives* are good candidates for capturing such learning.

Perhaps the social aspect of learning can be appropriately described as *crossing a gap*,[24] towards some information created or possessed by another person, as part of our motivation to better understand a situation. This is just one step, but it is a crucial one. When we are learning, we are constructing a meaningful relationship with what we are learning, sometimes mediated by a person or other medium, such as a book or a teacher. A teacher or a collaborator each act as both the bridge and the flashlight leading to the information, and as trustworthy companions. In other words, they all are aspects of the *structure* of the learning situation. When we relate to ideas, this allows us to engage in deeper reflection when the meanings we construct relate to more and perhaps more abstract ideas. This is called *knowledge building*.[25]

All of this may sound quite open and vague; but this is deliberate on our part, in order to preserve the idea that learning and situations are dynamic. For example, what does it mean to say we have learned to fight with a sword? What of that complicated skill is learned and to what extent? Can we describe what that skill consists of, *exactly*? The answer lies in that little word at the end: 'exactly'. And the answer is: no. We do not know exactly what it means to fight with a sword, but we know more or less, who is better at it, and some things that it is not. We can tell very personal stories involving sword fighting. Most importantly, we know *what it is used for*. This means that we are able to recognise similar structures in different situations of sword fighting. In the times of the Samurai, sword fighting was a great skill, to be acquired after long study, usually with several masters. These had mastered the skill, and also were masters in teaching, and they understood that mastery of sword fighting is linked to ways of seeing, experiencing and being in the world. A recent(!) re-edition of a Samurai manual on sword fighting[26] does not discuss the sword, or fighting, at all! Learning with a master was more than learning of facts and parts of a skill, it was initiation into a way of being. One could say that the learner was initiated into *a relationship with what to learn*. This was often called an art, rather than a skill. Most importantly, the science of sword fighting evolved as far as it did since it relates to universal wisdom. For more down to earth characters, it may be sufficient to chop off the enemy's head.

Could these masters then explain what sword fighting was about? Definitely not in one sentence or tweet, as would be required today. They would probably be able to generate highly abstract or spiritual descriptions or examples, or maybe great narratives, which would clarify how to behave and what to think. They would be able to recognise the *development of the learner* over time, and perhaps describe some of the features of that development. Every learner would develop in different ways, as such development also relates to *what the learner brings to the learning activity and experience*. In a way, this is design-based teaching, teaching adapted to what happens during the learning process.[27] The solution to such predicaments by many scientists and educationalists is this: make a test. A test is always normative; it is a choice of what is considered right, or good. Moreover, it is a temporary construct, restricted to norms and developments at the moment the test was conceived, even if it was statistically validated to the highest level.

> It took quite some time before the Samurai were able to read the village layout in terms of necessary defence structures. The help of the villagers was gratefully acknowledged. The villagers were also taught the skills of fighting with various weapons. Samurai were excellent sword fighters, and some of them were good with bow and arrow, but the farmers, even after some training, still preferred to use sharp stick for inflicting damage on their enemies.

> The stick was like an additional limb to them, supporting their work in the fields, their walking on different hilly slopes, or for guiding their animals. Using swords was unfamiliar to them. The skills that improved most involved using sticks for various purposes, defensive as well as offensive. Explanations by the Samurai on the assets of swords did not have much impact.

This example makes three things clear: first, learning is not always very concrete and specific, it is holistic; and what we learn is hard to explain and difficult to control. We do not know precisely what we know or what we have learned; but with serious effort, we may designate what we think it is about, more or less. The second thing we should be aware of from the above discussion is that there is a time dimension involved: *learning takes more or less time*, and it happens along several planes at the same time.[28] And, as you may have guessed, this timescale is very hard to specify. Apprentice-samurai stay with their master until mastery, or when the master has nothing to teach them anymore, which may take years. The time it takes to learn depends on how we delimit the learning activity – for example, short-term learning of what is there at the present time, or single ideas or concepts, as often happens in school contexts, or long-term learning as is involved in various types of mastery of the sword. And the third aspect is this: even individual learning involves a relationship with the learning material. This is not as simple as being motivated to learn. It is very specific, it is about what the learning materials mean to us, and reflection is about the meaning we can make out of the learning materials (as part of a meaningful activity) rising above what we already know and what has happened in a specific context.

The role of time in learning can be captured by projecting it in terms of *trajectories*. Look at the picture shown in Figure 7.2 (a *chronophoto-graph*, a collection of photos with the same frame taken with a stationary camera during a certain amount of time[29]), of the trajectory of birds, flying in the air above the Emporda wetlands in Cataluña.[30] The picture does not show a single trajectory, it shows several different intersecting trajectories, perhaps by several birds. This particular set of trajectories display flexible progressions over time, subjected to various influences, such as thermal and wind. Similarly, learning trajectories depict paths (progressions of understanding, but not necessarily in some desired direction) of meaning making about a particular topic or situation over time, with different durations, often still ongoing. The concept is very useful to grasp that in order to understand some activity, we may need to know something about its development over time. It also makes clear that although they represent development, trajectories are constructed *ad hoc*, that is, after we have decided what they are a trajectory *of*.

# COLLABORATING AND LEARNING 69

FIGURE 7.2  An ornithography, symbolising intersecting learning trajectories. An ornithography captures in a single time frame the invisible shapes that birds generate when flying, showing their intersecting trajectories. (Picture by Xavi Bou)

Learning always is part of a context or situation; but it is also part of several developmental trajectories. Some scientists argue that intersecting trajectories provide the greatest opportunities for deep learning.[31]

Does that answer the question of what we learn? No, it still does not. We will also not get the answer by classifying things (as in a taxonomy: animals, birds, robins), or producing a learning taxonomy (for example: facts, relations, concepts, inferences, etc.). These are concepts, created for the sake of clarification, with diverse meanings in different situations. It is somewhat helpful to apply a participatory definition, that what we learn is revealed as knowing how to act in meaningful situations (such as fighting with a sword when thieves try to steal our crop, or, more ambitiously; fighting together with Samurai; or knowing how to participate in the network of the powerful people in this world). How we act and why we act may reveal what we know.

Learning can be described as part of social action contributing to developmental trajectories of meaning making in the world. Here we do not distinguish depth or superficiality, but rather integration of ideas for 'higher' understanding. We may become wiser when we grow older, as a consequence of many interactions in different situations. We understand our experiences more easily because we are more able to create and relate to structural affordances. Obviously, such relationships are perspectives: there may be different things to learn in the same situation. If we want to understand what people learn, look at the situation they are in, and how they act to transform that situation.

We have discussed learning as integrated into meaningful activity in a social context, meaning being constructed at the intersection of many developmental trajectories, during which we reach out to ideas or people, thereby changing how we think and feel, our ideas and knowledge. Essentially, this already implies looking at learning from the point of view of social relations and structures (and not from a biological viewpoint, for example). What we learn depends on our views of the situation, that is, our angle of perception in a context. We could say that the views are more important than what we actually learn. Learning can be supported when people we trust or objects we understand show us when and what to reach out for in a complex environment: this is the structure. What we learn is to better exploit our resources in that situation (such as language, objects, other people) for goal directed activities.

## 2   Conditions for Collaborative Learning

| | |
|---|---|
| Context: | A group of Italian high school students is discussing the possible location of a new museum in their region. What the museum will display is still open for discussion. They have been asked (by the teacher) to use statistical data to support their proposals. |
| A: | I had a look at the list of museums present in Caserta province. I would say let's focus on the city of Caserta. I scrolled through and found only two museums present in Caserta, the Museum of contemporary art and the Michelangelo Museum, the others are all in the province. |
| B: | I know a little about Caserta and one of the main problems is the difficulty of entering the city. |
| A: | But there is the train station, I think this is a plus. |
| B: | Although as a territory it is very bicycle-friendly or to walk, because it has a flat surface. |
| A: | That is a fact. And it is already a centre visited by tourists and residents on site, so a nice museum would be just fine there. |
| C: | I too would vote for Caserta centre because also from the population data it appears to be one of the most densely populated areas, so it's already a plus for attracting tourists. We can check out the municipalities with more than 15,000 inhabitants. In my opinion we should choose between these because municipalities with fewer inhabitants are unlikely to attract large flows of visitors. |

Most conversation is cooperative. Taken as actions, actors build new action by selectively reusing resources provided by a prior action (sometimes called a *substrate*).[32] The linguist Charles Goodwin gives a simple example of this:

*Tony*: Why don't you get out of my yard.
*Chopper*: Why don't you *make me* get out of the yard.

From the example we can see some structure (and wording) being preserved, and something new is built within that structure. It is not about the repeating of words, but it is about a fundamental feature of all human action, which is to build on previous action, allowing for human culture and knowledge to accumulate in a systematic fashion.[33] A current substrate organises coherence by gathering together a limited collection of specific actions now in progress. Participants actively use them to build, in concert with each other, subsequent meaning and action that emerge coherently from what just gone before and provides materials for the construction of what will happen next. This is not only by using language, it can be by many sign systems, such as gesture and movement: an actor has many semiotic resources available.

This building on what is there is always a selection amongst various options. There seem to be more options when we act together. When doing things together, we need to coordinate, listen and speak, act, share, initiate and react towards and with the others. These others can be people we like (or like less) and be more or less familiar to work with, such as in professional contexts. As we have seen in previous chapters, many things happen during collaboration, and it rarely is a direct trajectory towards carefully planned goals. We may now understand why, and why life is like that. In fact, many things we learn, alone or together with others, are not constructive at all, or not all the time. We may learn how to avoid confrontation, for example, with dominant parents. Or someone might tell us that we are becoming a politician.

What we have been calling collaboration is more than building on actions of others, immediately or from the past. Let us remind ourselves what that means first: collaborating means people working together (1) as equals, (2) with the objective of shared meaning making, (3) under conditions of mutual respect and consideration (see Chapter 1 of this book). Concerning knowledge, the main affordances of collaborative situations for learning are in the greater availability of ideas and knowledge, when participants compensate for each other's weaknesses, add to ideas to make an issue clear, or elaborate ideas to give them more precision, depth and extension. People know different things and have different skills. Effectively joining forces may obviously serve the common cause; and participants will be sharing ideas and learn from that during the process. But the point is this: greater availability of resources and the requirement of joint exploitation of them does not tell us how to use those resources together. Building on what others do, engaging in mindful dialogue, undertaking respectful action, does not just happen: it requires agency and motivation to figure out how to do it.

> The Samurai and the villagers are slowly getting used to each other. This started by tolerating each other, and by engaging in some joint activity. Mutual understanding was growing, at least within the joint objective of defending the village. What helped was that one of the Samurai decided to sleep in one of the villager's houses, together with the family. It also helped that another samurai, who was a decent, friendly man, got interested in one of the women in the village. Many bigger and smaller incidents helped too: it made the groups more aware of each other's predicaments, their assets and barriers, providing explanations for initially peculiar looking behaviour. In other words, parallel to their training and learning experiences, the groups built up a mutual relationship.

Whilst working together, another aspect of learning is when participants build up some type of *working relationship*, or set of ways of working together.[34] This can be a slow process. In a more abstract sense, participants may gradually learn to understand what their collaboration is about, and what their personal skills and preferences contribute to the group and its objectives. Hence, at the level of activities, *collaborative learning is at the same time learning to collaborate and the learning that takes place when we collaborate*.[35] In a broader sense, collaborative learning may be defined as learning how to participate in communities of people, friends, colleagues, people with the same profession, or people sharing similar goals. In other words, it involves understanding *collaborative situations* in the world.[36]

What about striving to achieve shared objectives? We saw that the Samurai and the farmers had the shared objective of chasing the bandits from the village, and maybe even killing them. This idea was sufficiently shared as a starting point for collaboration. What the participants learned came from the activities as they were developed as a consequence. This could be about fighting techniques, preparing for a fight, building artefacts to defend the village, dealing with various uncertainties, with each other, etc. Calling some of this collaborative and the rest individual is an academic exercise. We prefer calling it all collaborative, as it involves *deliberate* acting and dealing with other people. The term 'deliberate' refers to the joint objective, not to planning the whole activity. Planning is often a part of an activity that is not collaborative at all.

In other contexts, sharing objectives may be the goal of the whole collaborative activity. In writing a proposal for a joint research project, for example, participants often ponder for a long time about the shared objectives and outcomes of such a project. The shared goal of a collaborative activity can be figuring out what the joint goals for future collaboration can be. Or, to turn it the other way around, in collaboration we have to look for what is shared in order to proceed. We always do.

Why is mutual respect an explicit criterion? It is because without it, there will be insufficient interest in each other for anything meaningful to evolve. Moreover, emotions may become tensions that are hard to reconcile when there is insufficient respect or consideration. Whilst there are important theories stressing the resolution of (socio-)cognitive conflict as a motor for learning,[37] in the case of collaboration this requires a group that is able to handle the tensions resulting from such conflict. Mutual respect can evolve from such endeavours, leading to trust between participants, and a greater ability of the group to deal with conflicts.[38]

There is another crucial aspect of collaborative learning that is less present in individual learning; and we call this the capacity to act: *agency*. As we have seen in our personal life stories on many occasions, collaboration often is action and the fine-tuning of such actions. This cannot be done by reflection alone: it requires action, knowing when to act, and what action to perform. It is this requirement for multiple types of agency that makes collaboration and collaborative learning so difficult, on the one hand, and so potentially powerful and rich, on the other. For individual small children, most natural learning is about understanding particular situations by experiencing the consequences of deliberate action within those situations. Agency does not only mean physical action, it can also mean being active in *dialogue*, by proposing, arguing, selecting, directing, etc. The crucial thing to realise here is that the agentive view sees learning as active rather than passive, and learning to be a function of our internal stories rather than of what comes in from the outside. So, how participants view their collaboration is crucial for the collaborative learning that takes place.[39]

## 3    School Learning

As we have discussed it so far, in our lives, most learning has been participatory and situated: we do not learn because we are being told, we simply learn. In the institution called school, we learn for the future, for becoming our own masters, and what we learn is supposed to be carefully designed. As a consequence, the situation of learning at school is different from the (presumably later) situation of application of the assumed new knowledge. School learning is a situation-transcending activity.[40]

At the same time, school is a culture in itself. Within the vaguely specified view on learning we described above, school cultures are characterised by very specific choices about what, how, and when we learn. These choices necessarily restrict much of what we learn to what can be designed controlled and evaluated. At least, that is what many educators think. In fact, children at school learn much more and many different things during their school careers than what a curriculum prescribes. Some of these things are good, others are less

> Context: A classroom of 23 4–5-year olds. The teacher (male) is leading a dialogue about the days of the week.
> ZIN *enters the classroom; all others are already sitting in a half circle:*
> Teacher: Hi ZIN, good you are joining us! (*he continues his discourse*).
> ZIN *does not reply, sits down next to another boy.*
> AZR (*plucking at her dress and looking around when the teacher looks at her*).
> Teacher: What day, IWA, comes after Sunday? (*He puts his hand on* IWA's *shoulder when he mentions his first name*).
> IWA (*when he is touched, he turns his head towards the teacher, but does not look at him. Then he turns his head in the direction of the calendar the teacher has positioned in front of the classroom, and speaks*): Monday.
> *The teacher then asks what to do when the figure on the table of days goes down.*
> AZR *raises her finger, with her T-shirt in her mouth. The teacher ignores her.*
> MAR *is addressed and gives the correct answer.*
> AZR: That is what I wanted to say huh! (*She drops her arm and looks at the floor*)
> Teacher: If you know what month that is ....
> IWA *quickly raises his arm.*
> Teacher: ... you will now stand on your chairs (*starts counting down from 5*).
> IWA *is the first to stand on his chair.*
> AZR *looks at the others and then also stands on her chair.*
> ZIN *tries to climb on his chair twice, backs down, and then stands on his chair at his third attempt.*
> HIK *stands on her chair when the counting is over.*
> MAR *remains seated.*
> HIK *and* ZIN *sit down immediately after* JIT *has provided the correct answer.*
> IWA *also sits down.*
> AZR *is the only one who remains standing while the rest sits. She looks around and finally sits down.*

good, and much is lacking. In other words, there is a problem with transcending the situation of school learning because learners are merely involved in dealing with the school culture. At the same time, learners are involved in other cultures, at home, on the street, in interactions with peers outside the school.

A main issue in school learning is that of the role of the teacher. People seem to agree that we need good teachers, but it is not obvious to most people what this means. We do not think that the main role of teachers is to tell us what to learn, thus turning us into passive learners. We think that the role of the teacher is to orchestrate and support student learning and autonomy, preferably by dialogue and collaboration, focused on student agency. In most forms of current education, primary, secondary or even tertiary, we do not see the relationship between teacher and student as collaborative, simply because it is not equal. Instead of a collaborator, the teacher is the director of all activity, the instructor explaining what to do and how to do it, and the evaluator of what students do.[41]

In more advanced educational settings, the teacher can also be the moderator or coach of student activity: standing on the side, trying to support student learning, not by providing the answers, but by nudging, and hinting, or with brief interventions aimed at increasing students' understanding of relevant aspects of the learning situation. If the current mainstream form of teaching as transmitting knowledge is that important, then students need to learn to teach as well, in order to understand the teaching-learning situation in a similar way as the teacher, and as a consequence, develop the collaborative skills to make shared stories about the same situation. One crucial step for this would be for teachers to negotiate with the students about assignments and their goals. This may very well bring out tensions, with the world, with the system, with the teacher. When handled diligently, authentic tensions can be engines for learning.

The impact of school culture on children's learning is highly effective: students come to view learning as something to be told, having clear external rewards, subjected to evaluation by authority, and as a completely individual matter. However, in Bruner's words "the objective of skilled agency and collaboration in the study of the human condition is to achieve not unanimity, but more consciousness. And more consciousness always implies more diversity".[42]

What is the nature of collaboration developing under transmission/reception systems of education? For one thing, because emotions are not considered to be relevant, it is highly emotional, especially since participants are not supposed to reveal their anxiety, which is considered to be something to be overcome. On the other hand, positive emotions, such as enthusiasm and pleasure,[43] as well as display of agreement and confirmation of the others' actions, are valued as signals of good collaboration. A number of other characteristics stand out.

Students engaged in collaborative activity in a classroom setting tend to focus on solutions rather than on understanding. They are not in *design mode*, but in belief mode.[44] A problem solved is one problem less, irrespective if the students understand the solution or not. Time constraints are enormously important: when time is nearly up, students tend to accept any solution as useful. The main concern becomes what they can get away with rather than good understanding. This applies to all forms of education, even at universities. A good teacher should always carefully consider the nature of the student solution. It should not have come from the teacher's mouth.

Also, students are hesitant to enter into meaningful joint discussion, or even to argue together. This applies to students who know each other well, and to students who are put together for the sake of the assignment. Rather, students divide up the tasks, so each can work on an individual piece of the puzzle, which pieces are then joined together in a later phase. This way of working we called *cooperation*: students work on parts of the same task, but each as an individual. This often makes sense, since one should not have to go over every detail together; and people differ in knowledge and in other respects, for example in their time constraints. What is avoided is not deepening understanding, but the intensity and anxiety of working together. In traditional education, this is considered as efficient practice and it is not criticised at all. Obviously, the cost is a lack of depth of understanding, of the domain, but also less knowledge of collaboration itself. One thing a good teacher could do is to check joint collaboration.

A third main characteristic of collaboration in traditional education is how students consider problems. While some theorists firmly believe that inquiry is about how students overcome impasses and difficulties,[45] students believe impasses are the proof that they are on the wrong track altogether.

So, what can we do about that?

It has been established by research that the autonomy-supportive style of teaching is far more effective than the control-oriented teaching strategy, with respect to development, motivation, engagement, performance and well-being of students.[46] The autonomy-supportive style focuses on developing student inner engagement and motivation, not by providing structure and answers, but by dialogue and collaboration. This means adopting student perspectives, welcoming student feelings, objections, personal ideas, and supporting students' doing things by themselves. It is clear that collaborative learning is part of this approach. We know it works and how it can be done.

## 4  Summarising Comments on Collaborative Learning

What did the farmers in *The Seven Samurai* learn from their collaboration? Not as much as they could have, since perception is always selection. One reason was their strong focus on the outcome. Much of what happened was interpreted in the light of effectiveness for chasing the bandits. Reflection on other things, such as collaboration itself, roles, skills, or people, was probably absent. With the clear goal in mind, some may have improved in fighting skill, but probably not in collaborative fighting skill, as stronger powers, the Samurai, had the main role in coordinating the actions, and doing the most difficult actions. The farmers were directed by and dependent on the Samurai. So, it is no real surprise that they did not learn as much, in spite of their collaborative activities.

School experiences are in some ways similar. The focus of the kids is on the outcome, but characteristically they lack the skills to produce a high-quality outcome. So, they simply act, one group better coordinated than the other. Differences exist in the attempts of the teacher to leave the autonomy of the kids intact. Also, where the farmers may have listened attentively to what the Samurai had to say, kids grow up to be less interested. Kids expect to be told what to do. This *mode* makes them less receptive to the resources in the situations, in the same way as the farmers who expected to be led by the Samurai.

For more effective coaching of collaboration it would be wise for teachers to know the children better, so they can interpret their actions more appropriately. But the main message of this chapter is this: the forms of collaboration we would like to see in educational contexts, supporting collaborative learning, do not simply happen by telling people to collaborate. We have seen many complexities of the collaborative process going wrong, therefore the collaboration for survival, as it has evolved in many animals,[47] does not serve as a sufficient basis for collaborative learning in our complex society.

### Notes

1. Have a look at the discussion about Vygotsky's (1986) idea that scientific concepts develop downwards and natural concepts upwards, as part of a study on natural versus institutional learning (Säljö, 1991).
2. According to the philosophers Deleuze and Guattari (1991, p. 10), philosophy is the discipline that consists in creating concepts; as such, its contemporary rivals are activities such as marketing and publicity that also make such a claim.

3  See the chapter "Toward a psychology of optimal experience" in Csikszentmihalyi (2014, pp. 209–226). In this framework, the focus is not on action, but on experience. In typical research inspired by this view, subjects are asked to fill out short questionnaires on their actions and feelings over long periods of time, for example during a week or more. The core question is "How happy are you feeling right now?"
4  See Bergsom (1896/2012).
5  Most of what is put forward on meaning making is inspired by Bruner (1990).
6  See Holzkamp (1992).
7  There is a special issue of the journal called *Mind, Culture and Activity* (2016, Vol. 23, 4) devoted to Vygotsky's concept of *perezhivanie*, which can be interpreted as standing for 'the whole experience', or 'the activity of experiencing'.
8  See Piaget (2015).
9  See Melander (2009).
10 Many scholars present evidence in favour of direct instruction over discovery learning, as if there was a competition between both. In school conditions, direct instruction should clearly win (see, for example, Klahr & Nigam, 2004).
11 See Bandura (1982), Scardamalia and Bereiter (1991), and Rajala (2016).
12 Of course, educational scientists do not agree about the use of testing in education. There's a review of a book by a policy maker who changed her views about testing in Ohana (2012). For another principled approach, see Matusov, Marjanovic-Shane, and Meacham (2016).
13 See Resnick (1987).
14 See Lave and Wenger (1991).
15 See Dreier (1999).
16 See Matusov (2009) and Cámara de la Fuente and Comas-Quinn (2016).
17 See Veerman, Andriessen, and Kanselaar (2000).
18 See Säljö (2009).
19 See Dewey (1910/1997).
20 Ibid.
21 See Ohlsson (2011).
22 See Wegerif (2007).
23 See Bohm (2013) and Wegerif, Boero, Andriessen, and Forman (2009).
24 See Biesta (2004).
25 See Bereiter (2005).
26 See Hatsumi (2005).
27 See Berliner (2002).
28 See Lemke (2000, 2001) and Lemke et al. (2007).
29 Chronophotography is defined as "a set of photographs of a moving object, taken for the purpose of recording and exhibiting successive phases of motion". The term chronophotography was coined by French physiologist Étienne-Jules Marey to

describe photographs of movement from which measurements could be taken and motion could be studied. It is derived from the Greek word χρόνος chrónos ("time") combined with photography (see Jay, 1972).
30 See http://www.xavibou.com/index.php/project/ornitographies/
31 See Furberg and Ludvigsen (2008).
32 See Goodwin (2013, 2018)
33 See Goodwin (2013, p. 9).
34 See Andriessen, Baker, and van der Puil (2011).
35 See Puntambekar (2006).
36 See Schwarz and Baker (2017).
37 See Perret-Clermont (1979) and Posner, Strike, Hewson, and Gertzog (1982).
38 See Engeström (2014).
39 A special issue of the journal *Learning, Culture and Social Interaction* (Vol. 10, September 2016), edited by Jenny Martin, Antti Rajala and Kristiina Kumpulainen, is devoted to the topic Agency and Learning: Researching Agency in Educational Interactions.
40 See Engeström (2016).
41 See Matusov, von Duyke, and Kayumova (2016).
42 See Bruner (1996, p. 97).
43 See Ehrenreich (2010).
44 See Scardamalia and Bereiter (2014) and Bereiter and Scardamalia (2014).
45 See Csikszentmihalyi (2014).
46 See Reeve (2009).
47 See De Waal (2010).

## References

Andriessen, J., Baker, M., & van der Puil, C. (2011). Socio-cognitive tension in collaborative working relations. In S. Ludvigsen, A. Lund, I. Rasmussen, & R. Säljö (Eds.), *Learning across sites: New tools, infrastructures and practices* (pp. 222–242). London: Routledge.

Bandura, A. (1982). Self-efficacy mechanism in human agency. *American Psychologist, 37*(2), 122.

Bereiter, C. (2005). *Education and mind in the knowledge age*. London: Routledge.

Bereiter, C., & Scardamalia, M. (2014). Knowledge building and knowledge creation: One concept, two hills to climb. In S. C. Tan, H. J. So, & J. Yeo (Eds.), *Knowledge creation in education* (pp. 35–52). Singapore: Springer.

Bergsom, H. (2012). *Matière et mémoire: essai sur la relation du corps à l'esprit*. Paris, France: Flammarion. (Original published 1896)

Berliner, D. C. (2002). Comment: Educational research: The hardest science of all. *Educational Researcher, 31*(8), 18–20.

Biesta, G. (2004). "Mind the gap!" Communication and the educational relation. *Counterpoints, 259*, 11–22.

Bohm, D. (2013). *On dialogue*. London: Routledge.

Bruner, J. S. (1990). *Acts of meaning*. Cambridge, MA: Harvard University Press.

Bruner, J. S. (1996). *The culture of education* (p. 97). Cambridge, MA: Harvard University Press.

Cámara de la Fuente, L., & Comas-Quinn, A. (2016). *Situated learning in open communities: The TED open translation project*. Cambridge: OpenBook Publishers.

Csikszentmihalyi, M. (2014). *Flow and the foundations of positive psychology*. Dordrecht: Springer.

Deleuze, G., & Guattari, F. (1991). *Qu'est-ce que la philosophie*. Paris, France: Les Éditions de Minuit.

De Waal, F. (2010). *The age of empathy: Nature's lessons for a kinder society*. New York, NY: Broadway Books.

Dewey, J. (1997). *How we think*. North Chelmsford, MA: Courier Corporation. (Original published 1910)

Dreier, O. (1999). Personal trajectories of participation across contexts of social practice. *Outlines. Critical Practice Studies, 1*(1), 5–32.

Ehrenreich, B. (2010). *Smile or die: How positive thinking fooled America and the world*. London: Granta Books.

Engeström, Y. (2014). *Learning by expanding*. Cambridge: Cambridge University Press.

Engeström, Y. (2016). *Studies in expansive learning: Learning what is not yet there*. Cambridge: Cambridge University Press.

Furberg, A., & Ludvigsen, S. (2008). Students' meaning-making of socio-scientific issues in computer mediated settings: Exploring learning through interaction trajectories. *International Journal of Science Education, 30*(13), 1775–1799.

Goodwin, C. (2013). The co-operative, transformative organization of human action and knowledge. *Journal of Pragmatics, 46*(1), 8–23.

Goodwin, C. (2018). *Co-operative action*. Cambridge: Cambridge University Press.

Hatsumi, M. (2005). *Japanese sword fighting: Secrets of the samurai*. Tokyo: Kodansha International.

Holzkamp, K. (1992). On doing psychology critically. *Theory & Psychology, 2*(2), 193–204.

Jay, B. (1972). *Eadweard Muybridge, the man who invented moving pictures*. New York, NY: Little, Brown, and Company.

Klahr, D., & Nigam, M. (2004). The equivalence of learning paths in early science instruction: Effects of direct instruction and discovery learning. *Psychological Science, 15*(10), 661–667.

Lave, J., & Wenger, E. (1991). *Situated learning: Legitimate peripheral participation.* Cambridge: Cambridge University Press.

Lemke, J. L. (2000). Across the scales of time: Artifacts, activities, and meanings in ecosocial systems. *Mind, Culture, and Activity, 7*(4), 273–290.

Lemke, J. L. (2001). The long and the short of it: Comments on multiple timescale studies of human activity. *The Journal of the Learning Sciences, 10*(1–2), 17–26.

Lemke, P., Ren, J., Alley, R. B., Allison, I., Carrasco, J., Flato, G., ... Zhang, T. (2007). Observations: Changes in snow, ice and frozen ground, climate change 2007: The physical science basis. In *Contribution of working group 1 to the fourth assessment report of the intergovernmental panel on climate change* (pp. 337–383). Cambridge: Cambridge University Press.

Matusov, E. (2009). *Journey into dialogic pedagogy.* Hauppauge, NY: Nova Science Publishers.

Matusov, E., Marjanovic-Shane, A., & Meacham, S. (2016). Pedagogical voyeurism: Dialogic critique of documentation and assessment of learning. *International Journal of Educational Psychology, 5*(1), 1–26.

Matusov, E., von Duyke, K., & Kayumova, S. (2016). Mapping concepts of agency in educational contexts. *Integrative Psychological and Behavioral Science, 50*(3), 420–446.

Melander, H. (2009). *Trajectories of learning: Embodied interaction in change* (Doctoral dissertation). Acta Universitatis Upsaliensis, Uppsala.

Ohana, C. (2012). The death and life of the great American school system by Diane Ravitch. *Journal of Educational Controversy, 6*(1), 26.

Ohlsson, S. (2011). *Deep learning: How the mind overrides experience.* Cambridge: Cambridge University Press.

Perret-Clermont, A.-N. (1979). *La construction de l'intelligence dans l'interaction sociale.* Bern, Switzerland: Peter Lang.

Piaget, J. (2015). *Structuralism* (Psychology revivals). London: Psychology Press.

Posner, G. J., Strike, K. A., Hewson, P. W., & Gertzog, W. A. (1982). Accommodation of a scientific conception: Toward a theory of conceptual change. *Science Education, 66*(2), 211–227.

Puntambekar, S. (2006). Analyzing collaborative interactions: Divergence, shared understanding and construction of knowledge. *Computers & Education, 47*(3), 332–351.

Rajala, A. (2016). *Toward an agency-centered pedagogy: A teacher's journey of expanding the context of school learning* (Doctoral dissertation). University of Helsinki, Helsinki.

Reeve, J. (2009). Why teachers adopt a controlling motivating style toward students and how they can become more autonomy supportive. *Educational Psychologist, 44*(3), 159–175.

Resnick, L. B. (1987). The 1987 presidential address: Learning in school and out. *Educational Researcher, 16*(9), 13–54.

Säljö, R. (1991). Learning and mediation: Fitting reality into a table. *Learning and Instruction, 1*(3), 261–272.

Säljö, R. (2009). Learning, theories of learning, and units of analysis in research. *Educational Psychologist, 44*(3), 202–208.

Scardamalia, M., & Bereiter, C. (1991). Higher levels of agency for children in knowledge building: A challenge for the design of new knowledge media. *The Journal of the Learning Sciences, 1*(1), 37–68.

Scardamalia, M., & Bereiter, C. (2014). Smart technology for self-organizing processes. *Smart Learning Environments, 1*(1), 1.

Schwarz, B. B., & Baker, M. J. (2017). *Dialogue, argumentation and education: History, theory and practice.* New York, NY: Cambridge University Press.

Veerman, A. L., Andriessen, J. E., & Kanselaar, G. (2000). Learning through synchronous electronic discussion. *Computers & Education, 34*(3), 269–290.

Wegerif, R. (2007). *Dialogic education and technology: Expanding the space of learning* (Vol. 7). Dordrecht: Springer Science & Business Media.

Wegerif, R., Boero, P., Andriessen, J., & Forman, E. (2009). A dialogue on dialogue and its place within education. In B. Schwarz, T. Dreyfus, & R. Hershkowitz (Eds.), *Transformation of knowledge through classroom interaction* (pp. 184–199). London: Routledge.

CHAPTER 8

# Collaborating and Arguing

At first thought, arguing seems incompatible with collaborating. But this is only under a particular way of seeing both, where collaboration is seen as friendly consensus, and argumentation as an unfriendly disagreement. In the English language, at least, the noun 'argument' can either mean a heated dispute ("we got into a terrible argument, and she left") or else, more neutrally, simply a statement (argument) designed to support another one, called a claim or thesis. This fits the definition used in the Monty Python 'argument clinic' sketch[1]: "an argument is a collective series of statements to establish a definite proposition".

As we shall explain, there are other ways to see both, which together underline a specific way of arguing that is just about as collaborative as one can get.

## 1  What Do We Call Argument(ation)?

But before explaining that, we think it might be useful to get some kind of working definition of what argument and argumentation are.[2] We will use the two more or less as synonyms, because an argumentation is just a chain of arguments designed to lead to a conclusion. There have been over two thousand years of reflexion on what argumentation is, beginning with "The philosopher", Aristotle. In recent centuries, mathematicians and logicians have tried to take over the idea of argumentation, basically reducing it to logical/mathematical demonstration – the type of thing you did at school, proving properties of triangles; or hackneyed examples like "Man is an animal, Jerry is a man, so Jerry is an animal" .... That is not what we're talking about here: we're talking about real argumentation, exchanged by people in dialogue; and we would claim that if you reduce it to 'pure reason', you miss a great deal.

We shall not try to review those past two thousand years of reflection on argumentation. For us, *argumentation is a means for trying to lead people to accept what you say*. A few words about that. In many European languages, the words argument and argumentation derive from ecclesiastical Latin (obviously, since those priests and monks were, for centuries, the only ones who could read and write). The word has two parts: the prefix 'argu-', that comes from the verb 'arguer', and the suffix '-mentum'. 'Arguer' means to point out or to bring to acknowledge. The suffix '-mentum' refers to the way, the means, the instrument or technique by which the verb to which it is attached is realised. Examples: 'monumentum' (a means for remembering), 'alimentum' (a means for nourishment), 'documentum' (a means for informing). So ... 'argumentum' *argumentation is ... a means for leading people to accept or acknowledge what you say*.[3] So far so good: but exactly what is that 'means', and why or when would you want to use it?[4]

## 2  When and Why to Argue

You would want to use the technique of argumentation when first, the person you're addressing does *not* – at least at first – accept what you say, and, second, when you *want* them to do so. But already, this becomes a bit mysterious, and the water deepens quickly: why would anyone want others to accept what they say? Why not just leave it at that, when they refuse, and walk away?

What *can* you argue about? You can argue, or rather people generally do argue, about things that are not clearly established and accepted by all. Things that *are* clearly established and accepted by all include things that are true by definition – such as '2 + 2 = 4', unless we decide to change the rules of arithmetic – or things that (unless you are a dogmatic Cartesian sceptic) are taken as obvious perceptual facts ("I am writing on a computer keyboard"), or that are established by scientific methods ("the holocaust existed"). Things that are not necessarily accepted by all include disputed hypotheses about the physical world ("the dinosaurs died out because of a meteor hitting the Earth") and many aspects of life in society ("if medical science would enable it, men should be able to bear and give birth to babies").

So, why argue, about things that can be or are generally argued about? Well ... because you, others, *care about the answer*, because you consider it important, and ... because whether what you argue about is accepted by others or not, is also important, in that it bears on social life, our life together. "Would Marine Le Pen be the best president of the French Republic or not?". That is a question that we care about, and the answer that would be given to it, collectively, would concern everyone, not just the French. So we will engage in argumentation about that question, and thereby strive to make others accept our view. Similarly, with general social questions, such as additives in food, use of nuclear power, and so on.

We argue because we care about the outcome of the argument. But, as we discuss below, there can be many other reasons for being interested enough in a question for being willing to argue about it.

## 3  What Is the Technique (of Argumentation)?

That is an easy question to answer: the technique involves either providing arguments (!), reasons for accepting or rejecting what is proposed, or else presenting the issue in a certain way such that it would be more or less acceptable. Suppose I wanted you to vote for Marine Le Pen (a horrible example, for us, and we certainly do not want that; but let's follow the example). What techniques could I use to get you to accept that she would be the best president?

Let's rule out first of all methods of coercion and violence, or the use of drugs, threats, etc.: that is an important point; the ecclesiastical Latin idea of argumentation took it for granted that it was a technique that involved only use of spoken or written *words*, texts, speeches, discourse, *language*, not other types of physical actions. So, ... I could produce an 'argument', a reason for accepting my view, such as "her economic policy will increase the salary of everyone". This would count as an argument (although the truth of the statement is not at all established) because of a particular link between it and what it is designed to make you accept: it will only work as an argument if you consider that getting more money is a good thing, and the general statement that "any action that produces good effects is a good action" (i.e. Le Pen's election would produce a good effect – more money for all – so it would be a good thing). This is the 'structural' approach to argumentation.[5] General statements, underlying the link between argument and claim, such as "actions that produce good effects should be performed", or "given them an inch, they'll take a mile", are what define 'types' of arguments (Aristotle called them 'topoi', from topos, place, as in the term 'commonplace' ideas).

There is the second aspect to the technique, which is not making isolated statements, but rather, representing things in a certain way. This is the 'discursive' approach to argumentation.[6] For example, someone might weave together a discourse on Marine Le Pen as 'a true defender of the French people', 'a fine mother' who nevertheless had a career as a barrister ('just a plain working mum'), and so on: such is the stuff of publicity and promotional videos. There is a subtle interplay between weaving such discursive threads, to represent things in a certain way, to persuade, and in putting forward reasons, arguments, in the attempt to convince, both of which aim at the other's acceptance.

Argumentation can occur in texts or speeches and it can also be an interactive affair, in dialogue between several people, each of whom argue in the sense described above, for and against their own and others' views. In is in this case – argumentation dialogue – that it can be seen as more or less collaborative.

So far, we have seen argument(ation) as an *individualistic* matter, where one tries to get another to acknowledge or accept some view. Before talking about collaborative argumentation, something more collective and two-way, let's look at how it can be un-collaborative, boring or, we would say, rather pointless for humankind.

## 4   Un-Collaborative Argumentation: Pitfalls

We think that some uses of argument are simply bad or pointless. Of course, that is a statement of our values, and it is not surprising that there can be either good or bad uses of a technique for producing words aiming at changing what others think. It depends, in part, on *what it is* that you want to make others accept, on the ethical value of that, but also on *how* you do so: the 'what' and the 'how'. But more generally, what we will call the pitfalls of argumentation relate to pursuing *individualistic* rather than *collective* aims: if Fred wants his group of friends to accept what he says about politics, then fine for Fred; but he is just wasting other people's time if he pursues aims that others don't care about at all.

One well-known case of an end and a means is called 'persuasion'. The end is to get others to accept, and the means are not always fair.

This is not considerate, except in some (Dutch sub-)cultures where telling what you think means taking people seriously. But as we often see or experienced in debates, argumentation does not always involve persuasion by means of correct arguments; it may involve putting forward fake ideas or 'facts' and it may involve strong rhetorical elements, that is, trying to persuade not by means of logic and reason, but by trying to impress, by using threatening language (*argumentum ad baculum*), or even, as sometimes happens in politics, enforcing a point of view by making the other side look foolish and stupid (*argumentum ad hominem*).

There is another possible pitfall of argumentation, which is that an orientation towards consensus, to being over considerate, may lead to superficial argumentation, where nothing is deepened at all. This depends on culture too. Some cultures, such as in Japan, emphasise group harmony ('wa'), with no overt interpersonal disagreement, and avoidance of self-assertion, within a strong social hierarchy. Others, such as in Israel, have a special form of socially ritualised talk, called 'dugri', meaning basically 'straight talking', intended for airing differences and getting to the bottom of the matter. It may be that both the antagonistic as well as the collaborative attitudes produce arguments that are either too personal or too obvious to make any sense. Argumentation is difficult because it requires a different motivation than the ordinary: we must be strongly motivated to advance our understanding (about the other, or about the domain) rather than trying to persuade, or even overrule, the other party. Once we understand what this motivation feels like, and what it is for, argumentation can be a powerful tool for learning and understanding, and a very collaborative one too.

For what problem is argumentation the solution? First, what it is *not* a solution for. In spite of what most people think, argumentation is not for convincing the other to share your opinion. Research has shown that such a goal leads to us supporting our own opinions, of which there are so many around, instead of backing up our opinions with data. People's personal opinions are rarely well developed in terms of elaborated ideas and warrants, but instead are based on emotions and on what others in the group are thinking (see Chapter 9). On many topics, people do not even have opinions. They make them up on the spot. Similarly, convincing the other during some debate does not always mean the other accepts what you say, (s)he may be bored or out of arguments.[7]

Nevertheless, people do have debates. But during such debates, they do not necessarily argue collaboratively, in the sense of jointly exploring pros and cons of a certain position, but instead, they present ideas reflecting their personal interpretations of the world. As a consequence, what we have is two simultaneous monologues, with participants alternating voices. Liberals cannot be argued out of their beliefs by a socialist, even though the latter may be right, from a particular point of view. People may change ideas, but rarely their fundamental beliefs, based on values, or: their interpretations of the world.

We think that argumentation is not, by definition, a means for persuading others: people may argue with no hope of convincing others, or even when they know that they agree. It is by argumentation, even the not very collaborative versions of it, that people may gradually understand their *own* interpretations of the world: they recognise what they think and feel. Argumentation comes after the facts, and does not serve to defend our own ideas. It does not help to defend our ideas in this way, because others do not necessarily attack them, they also present their own ideas. Persuasion only can be effective when the other is open to it, in other words, when the other is collaborative.

Do not think too badly of people's opinions: we cannot expect anything else from people trying to understand the complexities of their ever-changing environments and giving meaning to what happens when people go through life. This tells us at the same time not to think too highly about people's interpretations of the world. For many things we can only have simple interpretations, or none at all. Requiring opinions and arguments from people who barely had a chance or do not know how to understand a phenomenon does not make much sense.

So, why argue, in what way does it help us? We have given one answer already: it is to understand. To understand ourselves, to understand others, to understand the world. But we should not argue superficially, simply to confirm what we think, or for the sake of argument. We should engage in a serious attempt to clarify things, not for persuasion, but for understanding. Such is the problem of argumentation: it can help us in understanding the world if it is part of a serious dialogic inquiry about discovering where we stand with respect to various issues. These issues can be those of the past if we want to understand history. These issues can come from practice, if we want to understand how professionals think.

Why is argumentation so important for understanding? It is because it puts us on the track of integrating emotional and factual modes of reasoning and understanding. People have relevant feelings, based on their experiences, but those experiences may not be fully understood, which may be revealed and (partly) addressed by argumentation. And also, it is a track, a process whereby one utterance follows the other in a meaningful way, as is in a story where an event unfolds. Although *linearization* (the order of sentences in a text and also the order of words within sentences) can be difficult in written texts like the one we are writing now,[8] in collaborative dialogue participants can be deeply involved in a flow of jointly unfolding of ideas.

One comment about how professionals think is in order. It is often said that scientific argumentation is the ultimate form of argumentation, people should learn to argue like scientists. As long as that does not imply that we should argue like many scientists do (and we know that also scientists sometimes engage in strong persuasive language), we may understand this as meaning that argumentation should be an open effort towards understanding the world as part of a scientific enterprise. This enterprise is not looking for what is 'right' or 'true' in order to know what the world *is*, but rather it tries to understand interpretations: if this were true, what world view would fit with that? And: what does it mean to believe that X is true? Such questions touch the core of scientific argumentation and it is what we should strive for, as the philosopher Kant already told us. According to our interpretation, of course, with open-mindedness as a keystone.

## 5  Argumentation in the Real World: An Illustration

In some democracies, the system includes a process called a referendum. A referendum (in some countries synonymous with a plebiscite – or a vote on a ballot question) is a direct vote in which an entire electorate is asked to vote in favour or against a particular proposal. What is required for a person, or organisation to ask for such a plebiscite is to collect a sufficient number of signatures of people who support it to be organised. With current social media, this is relatively easy to do. After sufficient support has been established, national structures financially support organisations that want to campaign for or against the position the referendum asks to vote about. In the Netherlands, there recently was a vote about improving business relations between countries of the European Union and the Ukraine. In the UK, there was one about leaving the European Union entirely. As is always the case nowadays, the minimum number of votes is barely reached, and the voters who show up often vote against the position upheld by government. It always is a close finish, meaning that the verdict often only represents slightly more than 15% of the population.

What is the role of argumentation in such referenda? Some people are strongly in favour, and they have their opinions. The same for those who are against some position. As we know, opinions are not arguments. People can read or listen to argumentation in the media about the consequences of either position, even on the consequences of not voting at all. There we have learned that both issues (more business with Ukraine or the UK leaving the EU) are not simple at all, and even experts do not really agree on what will happen after a yes or no. Nevertheless, some people (slightly more than 30% of the population) vote. This vote is considered the output of an argumentative process, but is it?

What we want to say is this: if even in serious political participatory events argumentation is not frequently used even to defend an upheld position, then this defending of a position may not be the main goal of argumentation in such cases, and possibly in general. Asking for opinions may not be a good cause for a debate. Instead, it would be better that argumentation were about increasing our understanding of an issue. What is a good basis for a debate is the desire to close the gap between what we understand and what we need to understand, for example in order to make a decision. Our main thesis is that this can only happen if we collaborate, as the gap between interpretations can only be bridged if it is revealed, at least partly, what is there on the other side. If argumentation is not collaborative, the goal of joint exploration is not shared and the process will not lead to more understanding of the issue. It may lead to the understanding that the other will not reveal an opinion or relevant knowledge, or does not have any opinion or relevant knowledge at all. In other words, many outcomes of studies in which we study how people argue are a consequence of how argumentation is framed in those studies.

## 6  Collaborative Argumentation

We can now sum up what collaborative argumentation is, and why one might want to do it.[9] It basically involves a move from the 'I' and the 'you', to the 'we'. In other terms, it means not trying to use the technique of argumentation to impose what 'I' think, on 'you', but trying to use it to come to a decision, together, about what 'we' think and would be willing to accept. Sure, within that it's ok for there to be momentary lapses into individualism, when you just know you're right; but it's only of interest to push that if it would contribute to the 'we'.

Let's take again as an example, the question "should the UK leave the EU or not?", where Xavier says yes and Yolande says no. The individualistic technique of arguing would involve X providing arguments for Brexit, such as the money that would be saved, the good things that could be done with it, and so on, in an attempt to get Y to accept Brexit; all of which arguments Y could counter, and evoke the bad consequences for trade, and so on. What is the point of this? Most probably, the views of X and Y are not particularly sensitive to such practical arguments; it is more likely that their views are based on something else, that does not change as one does one's socks, called *values*. X probably has nationalistic values, Y probably those of sharing, and community, across Europe, its history and culture. So there is probably no point in trying to fundamentally change the other's view in the space of a discussion, but there might be an individualistic 'point' of each showing the other that they have every right not to change what they each think.

Could there be a collaborative version of this debate? To look back to Chapter 1 of this book, that would involve X and Y allowing each other the equal rights to express their views and arguments, showing some consideration for the other (such as not rejecting what they say out of hand) and, finally, some kind of co-construction, perhaps of a new, shared, way of seeing the question, each having at least understood what the other thinks. There would also perhaps be a small space for agreement on certain points, that it might surprise X and Y to discover. In collaborative argument, the question of (possibly) shared values is crucial. Within people who share values, they can disagree on specific points, but more easily co-construct a new shared view. Otherwise, it is more difficult.

Collaborative argumentation also involves a particular way of going about doing that, together, that we shall look into a little. Collaborative argumentation is not just about trading arguments and counter-arguments, it also involves other things, like asking for clarifications, but more importantly, it means *playing (the dialogue game) by the rules*. What are those rules? Everyone knows them, in fact. For example, everyone has seen or engaged in the childish game of "yes it is, no it isn't, 'tis, t'isn't", etc. And it does not get anyone anywhere, other than maintaining assertion of individuality. Just continuing to deny or assert doesn't enable the dialogue to get anywhere; so if your view is criticised, you're supposed to reply to that, with some kind of defense. Similarly, changing sides continually, vehemently attacking a view, then defending it, then back again, also makes things go round in a circle, as does quitting the game in the middle. So, if you do engage in collaborative argument, you agree to not waste other people's time and effort; you agree to give arguments for what you say, listen to the other, and try sincerely to reach some kind of agreed outcome.

To summarise, why do argumentation collaboratively, and why is it a particularly collaborative thing to do, as we said at the beginning of this chapter? You might want to do it, basically, because you believe in the values of mutual respect of collaboration, rather than in being individualistic ..., and – as we discuss in the next section – because you might get somewhere by doing that, in other words, you might *learn* something, about what other people think and about the very topic that you are debating with others. Collaborative argumentation is super-collaborative because it puts special demands on people, to not just walk away from others who disagree with them, to overcome selfishness, self-centredness or arrogance, to listen to others, to respect them, to take the risk that what you say will not be part of the collectively valid.

So what could you learn from collaborative argumentation, and how?

## 7     Arguing and Learning

There is something about arguing in a collaborative way that is good for very special types of learning. By that, we don't mean learning some kind of rhetorical general technique, the art of always being right; we mean learning about others, about yourself and about what it is you are debating.

Let's start with 'your self'. In arguing with others, in an open way, with genuine curiosity and awareness about what you are doing, you can come to a better understanding of yourself, about what you think, in a more coherent way, about particular issues that concern you. Because you have been willing to open up yourself to others, to difference, to diversity of views and criticism. Why would you want that? Who knows? Explanation and justification must stop somewhere, for limited mortals. But we think that many people will want to become the kind of person who wants to change, learn, evolve, in society; and engaging in collaborative argumentation is a good way to achieve that. If not: ok, stay in your solipsistic self-asserting world.

Now, what about learning about others? When people genuinely enter into collaborative argumentation, they put themselves at risk, the risk of receiving the approbation of others, since, if the dialogue is to have any point, they have to express themselves, their thoughts and feelings. Now, isn't that a beautiful thing, sharing such things with others? A vulnerable thing too. One of the things that characterises *Homo Sapiens* is an incredible degree of *diversity* between each of us, given the large part of incorporation into ourselves of individual experience of culture, whilst at the same time being the same, in biological and deontological senses. But if people do make that leap, opening themselves up to criticism, they can benefit from participating in the diversity of others, and maybe incorporate some of that into themselves. Argumentation means giving reasons, which requires delving into yourself, and expressing things in a particular way, which can be creative. In collaborative argumentation, each gives of themselves in this way, and each can profit from it. We, the authors, have both been university teachers. Every year, even if you the professor remain more or less the same, you have different students! And *always*, each year, one of them puts forward an idea you had never thought of. Need we say more? Collaborative argumentation means opening up oneself, exploring questions, together, in a free manner whilst being respectful to others. The leap into that requires courage to open up and gain together.

There is more. Argumentation between self-assertive individualists often means taking for and against stances. In collaborative argumentation, we learn to be more subtle, less binary; most important questions are not like that, we have to learn the degrees to which we might give our assent to some idea. And this means in some way becoming more generally open to the circulation of alternative discourses, views: becoming a 'CAP' (the invention of an acronym here is a bit of gentle humour), a 'Collaboratively Argumentative Person'.

Now the more mundane part: learning about the topic being debated. Suppose you're discussing, maybe over dinner, the latest humanoid robot, made in the image of Scarlett Johansson, and you think it's going too far, you can't see the point (other than some sick dehumanising sex toy), and a friend says don't be so closed minded, it's inexorable technological progress. That might be a fun discussion (see Figure 8.1). But, depending on what you and your friend know about robots, you might learn something about how they work, and you might even deepen your understanding of what it means to be human. You might also become acquainted with a whole range of arguments for or against robots and humanoid ones. In other words, you might broaden your understanding of the debate and deepen your understanding of the whole topic.[10]

COLLABORATING AND ARGUING 93

FIGURE 8.1   Discussing about a humanoid robot of Scarlett Johansson can a be learning experience (drawing by Roxane Oudart-Détienne)

In sum, collaborative argumentation is good for learning: about yourself, about others, and about the topic you are discussing. In the individualistic form of argumentation, you would probably be closed off to much of this, doggedly trying to push forward your own view, and closing off your mind to anything anyone else says. "How stupid", we would be tempted to say.

## 8   Coda

It is neither possible nor desirable to try to collaborate with everyone with whom you disagree, in order to construct some new way of seeing things. Think of obvious examples such as Holocaust deniers, or self-righteous propagators of fake news: these are people against whom one should simply fight, by all fair, democratic, rational and legal means. Because in those cases, there is no hope of receiving in return the respect you might offer them, in other words: collaboration. But if there does seem to be some common baseline of values, of humanity, then, even if you don't agree with someone, why not nevertheless try to collaborate with them, and go further together, rather than trying to push forward your own thing?

**Notes**

1 See https://www.youtube.com/watch?v=Lvcnx6-oGhA
2 The characterisation of argumentation that follows is based on a broad variety of research in modern argumentation theory. For that background, the reader will find the following works useful: van Eemeren, Grootendorst, and Snoeck Henkemans (1996) and Plantin (2018).
3 See Rigotti and Greco Morasso (2009).
4 See Russell (1927/1957).
5 See Toulmin (1958).
6 See Perelman and Olbrechts-Tyteca (1958).
7 See Stein and Miller (1991).
8 See Coirier, Andriessen, and Chanquoy (1999).
9 See Schwarz and Baker (2017).
10 See Baker, Andriessen, Lund, van Amelsvoort, and Quignard (2007).

**References**

Baker, M., Andriessen, J., Lund, K., van Amelsvoort, M., & Quignard, M. (2007). Rainbow: A framework for analysing computer-mediated pedagogical debates. *International Journal of Computer-Supported Collaborative Learning*, 2(2–3), 315–357. https://doi.org/10.1007/s11412-007-9022-4

Coirier, P., Andriessen, J. E. B., & Chanquoy, L. (1999). From planning to translating: The specificity of argumentative writing. In J. Andriessen & P. Coirier (Eds.), *Foundations of argumentative text processing* (pp. 1–28). Amsterdam: Amsterdam University Press.

Perelman, C., & Olbrechts-Tyteca, L. (1958). *Traité de l'argumentation. La nouvelle rhétorique*. Brussels, Belgium: Editions de L'université de Bruxelles.

Plantin, C. (2018). *Dictionary of argumentation: An introduction to argumentation studies*. Milton Keynes: College Publications.

Rigotti, E., & Greco Morasso, S. (2009). Argumentation as an object of interest and as a social and cultural resource. In N. Muller Mirza & A.-N. Perret-Clermont (Eds.), *Argumentation and education: Theoretical foundations and practices* (pp. 9–66). New York, NY: Springer.

Russell, B. (1957). *Why I am not a Christian: and other essays on religion and related subjects*. New York, NY: Allen & Unwin. (Original published 1927)

Schwarz, B. B., & Baker, M. J. (2017). *Dialogue, argumentation and education: History, theory and practice*. New York, NY: Cambridge University Press.

Stein, N. L., & Miller, C. A. (1991). I win – you lose: The development of argumentative thinking. In J. F. Voss, D. N. Perkins, & J. W. Segal (Eds.), *Informal reasoning and education* (pp. 265–290). Hillsdale, NJ: Lawrence Erlbaum Associates.

Toulmin, S. (1958). *The uses of argument.* Cambridge: Cambridge University Press.

van Eemeren, F. H., Grootendorst, R., & Snoeck Henkemans, F. (1996). *Fundamentals of argumentation theory: A handbook of historical backgrounds and contemporary developments.* Mahwah, NJ: Lawrence Erlbaum Associates.

CHAPTER 9

# How It Feels to Collaborate

In this chapter we discuss the role of emotions in collaboration, especially in relation to its dimensions that we have distinguished in Chapter 1: equality, sharing, and consideration.

How does it feel to collaborate?[1] Consider the experience of playing music together, especially when all do their best and succeed in sounding original and coherent, by carefully relating to what the others are playing. It feels highly satisfying to be involved in a joint activity in which all are bringing out their very best, and, as a consequence, being in a flow rising above individual expectations and capabilities. Achieving such a level of quality requires investing great time and effort in playing together, in addition to individual accomplishment. Participating in a successful joint experience must therefore be highly rewarding, especially when the success came unexpectedly, and individuals feel that their own contributions made a difference.

Being successful as an individual can be satisfying as well. The successful subject may feel competent, satisfied, recognised as an expert, or finally accepted as a human being by members of the family. An accomplished individual can make other people happy, after success has been achieved, when expertise is shared or shown. However, feelings of success achieved in actual collaboration may be different.

Humans have a capacity for intersubjectivity, defined as the ability to understand the minds of others,[2] which relates to the feeling (and motivation) of being in coordination with others.[3] It may also be that understanding of individual emotions has intersubjective roots. There is the possibility that being together is more natural than being alone. Some important psychological theories suppose that individual understanding is derived from what has initially happened on the social plane, in the presence of (significant) others.[4] From early childhood onwards, people learn to understand their individual emotions by interpreting those of others within a particular familiar context. Pleasure, disappointment, anger, first experienced as physiological states, are part of intersubjective experiences and are then understood as emotions which are more or less natural or acceptable in these contexts.[5]

Being together can be a strong motivation for many people. Being alone often is regarded as less pleasant or to be avoided. Nevertheless, in society, and especially in professional contexts, individual achievements are highly valued, directly related to praise, individual promotion, and more money. Collective improvement, reward or promotion is less institutionalised, except perhaps in some team sports. But even there, only the real stars (and their expert negotiators) receive big money. These days, in highly achieving companies, ambitious individuals who desire to climb within the system are in competition with their nearest colleagues, with whom they share many interests at the same time. This may look like friendly behaviour in the presence of those colleagues, but may also be associated with self-promotion and even stabbing other colleagues in the back when they are not present. It looks like career achievement has an emotional price tag: learning to live with the complexity of feelings associated with professional activity. Our individual life stories (Chapter 2) are full of such examples.

Feelings in interaction are of different kinds, positive as well as more negative ones, at the same time. By positive we mean (here) feelings of pleasure, liking, enjoying the activity and the challenge, working with the others, etc. By negative we mean (here) anxiety about not knowing what to do, not knowing the answer, not really knowing what to expect from the others, time constraints, etc. Or even worse, how to work collaboratively with individuals who we do not even like or trust? Feelings are complex, having different sources (personal, historical, situational and/or relational) and all of these at the same time. Feelings differ in strength; people differ in the degree to which they are sensitive to them and to what extent they are led by their emotions. Overcoming negative feelings about others is not always negative in collaboration, or in professional life. Within any timescale, feelings change and evolve in nature and in strength, and they are diffuse rather than stable. To paraphrase the 19th century founding father of psychology, William James: *No one ever had a simple emotion by itself. Consciousness, from our natal day, is of a teeming multiplicity of objects and relations, and what we call simple sensations are results of discriminative attention.*[6] Our emotions may belong to 'higher' attitudes and principles, such as pride, sense of nobility, chivalry, etc. We think that understanding and regulating feelings that arise during collaboration is a crucial quality of good collaborators. Understanding oneself, to some extent, seems a prerequisite that we will not go into here. Just as in individual learning, groups can develop sensitivity for their feelings, as well as a sense of what emotional stability for the group means and looks like.

## 1 An Example of Emotions and Emotional Regulation

Below, we see a short episode of a discussion between professionals, a group of 13 participants sitting around a large table. Two of them are researchers who do not participate in the discussion. Five of them are public administrators of a medium to large municipality, working for the Department of Social Welfare and Employment. They have been asked by their managers to investigate the use of a technology platform that would allow searching, viewing and discussing open data (statistical information) on issues pertaining to their domain: job seekers, employability, policy making, and many others. Another five are local employers, who have been invited to discuss possibilities for collaboration with the Department on the topic of resolving issues of unemployment. With the researchers, who are responsible for dealing with user needs in the design of the technology platform, the group has agreed to discuss their ideas for using such a platform. In this particular session, the group is asked to discuss the following topic: *People over 50 who lose their job currently remain unemployed longer (compared to younger job seekers), so their distance from the labour market is increasing. How can public administrators and employers together think of creative solutions to this problem, exploiting open data?* The numbered paragraphs below are the first contributions to the discussion. PA refers to public administrators, EM to employers, the index (e.g. PA1) refers to particular individuals. PA2 is the chair of the meeting. After the example, we will comment on some of the emotional and collaborative characteristics of this discussion.

1. PA1: By coincidence, this afternoon I participated in the Employer Service Centre Management Team and there we presented a little plan for doing something about the 50+ issue. If we look at our city then you see that the percentage of older than 50 on welfare really is increasing quite substantially. It is now already about 30 percent. And when I look at the return from welfare, then the percentage of return by the elderly is only 10 percent and that is much much lower compared to the other age groups.
2. EM1: Just an intervening question from me: 30 percent, then the other 30 percent is under 50, and you still need to work 17 years after 50, so 2 times 17 is 34, so then you start with the working population, so that is in fact an equal division.
3. PA1: No, because relatively few younger people are on social benefits and the category 27–50 is about 45–50%
4. PA2: You say that success is lower than the others and that makes it worse.
5. PA1: Yes, that is significant.
6. PA2: That's what makes it so bad. If I am correct the return of not above 50 is about 60–75 percent and the return above 50 is 10 percent, so that is considerable!

HOW IT FEELS TO COLLABORATE 99

7. EM1: Within a certain period or never anymore?
8. PA1: Well, you should never say never, but we see the number of people over 50 who do not return is simply increasing.
9. EM1: And then you talk about welfare? (*Note: welfare is a minimal state allowance received after two years without a job*)
10. PA1: Then you are talking about welfare.
11. EM1: So that already is after two years?
12. PA1: That already is after two years without a job.
13. EM2: So, data can help indeed in such cases, such as how is the situation in other municipalities, and if there is return, to which jobs do people go, and what precedes this return, training or not, or do they find jobs in their own sector?

PA1 starts the discussion. He establishes being part of the Department management team (important), which is active, having made a (little) plan. This part of his contribution is meant for PA1 to look competent and active. The second part of his contribution confirms the importance of the issue of elderly unemployment. This importance is established by presenting figures. Note the use of the terms *quite substantially, it now already is*, and *that is much much lower*. We conjecture that this will make the speaker appear serious and committed.

Contribution number 2 is by an employer. He tries to attack the interpretation of the figures. In our view on emotions, this also often means attacking the previous speaker, at least with respect to his authority, and maybe concerning other ideas of competence this speaker tried to display.

Note that the emotion is wrapped up in the content. The speaker does not say: "I feel you are not a reliable interpreter of figures", or even "you stupid arrogant administrator", but this may be an implication.

The discussion continues between these two protagonists, until contribution 12. PA1 is at some point supported by PA2 (in contributions 4 and 6). The exchange looks polite, but behind the considerateness, we may suppose some emotions. For one, it was part of general knowledge that elderly unemployed have more problems on the job market, so why attack that assumption? Also, when it appears that, after 6, EM1 has to concede, he instead raises more doubt, in 7, 9, and 11, by asking for additional confirmation. This may serve asserting his position in opposition to the public administrator.

This short discussion can also be taken as an argument such that open data can be useful. This is recognised by EM2, in a brilliant contribution (13). Not only does it return to the main question, illustrating the need for using open data, it also serves to reconciliate the two parties, and, at the same time, to define possible elaborations of the issue. This is a collaborative move, because it shows awareness of the group and its objective. Also, it regulates the discussion to proceed to more productive grounds. And it is a considerate move, because it is conciliatory in style rather than involving blaming or contradicting someone. This may lead to a reduction of tension in the group, and between the two antagonists. It should be noted that PA1 remains rather distant during the rest of the discussion, whilst EM1 has more of these directed interventions in later stages.

## 2   Diversity and Equality

Pleasure may not be the only socio-affective experience of collaboration. The intersubjective domain involves many emotions, especially in the relational realm. One collaborates differently with different people, and also the attendant emotions differ. When I [Jerry] asked my children, then at high school age, what they thought about collaborating with their peers, their first reaction was negative, because there were many of their classmates that they definitely did not want to work with. Some of them were not nice as people, and very often these other students were considered not to be good collaborators.

Differences in knowledge, motivation or personal characteristics between people can cause negative feelings about collaboration. These feelings are based on experience. One aspect of this experience is in the negative attitudes about school, in which many students, especially boys, think it is uncool to be serious about schoolwork. Collaboration between several students requires them to align in terms of attitudes about the importance of their collaboration. This also asks them to agree about the importance of schoolwork. If the team fails, even when there are competent and constructive members, these competent members are blamed for the failure as well. This may be one reason why collaborative learning in school contexts is often so unpopular.

Collaboration with others, involving different skills, knowledge and attitudes, is often not seen as a challenge by school students, but rather as something to be avoided. One's competence and efforts are seen as being affected by less motivated or less competent members. Collaborative efforts and collaborative achievements are rarely recognised in professional and school contexts.

Dealing with emotions in the context of diversity and equality is one of the most sensitive issues of contemporary times. The example above is a very moderate case of a difference between members of two communities: public administrators and employers. These two communities have different, albeit overlapping goals. Not only are their goals different, but also their styles of discussion, as the example has demonstrated. The public administrator likes to stick to the facts, and he may have been used to his community accepting his authority in that respect. The employer may be used to directly addressing issues, and to doubt all references to figures, as in his experience these may be strongly politically motivated. It is hard to say that a single discussion like this will serve to overcome the many differences that characterise the two communities. However, what we claim could happen when these participants continue to collaborate over extended periods of time, discussing various issues, is that their mutual understanding is increased. What we cannot claim is the extent to which this was already the case. What could have evolved into an effective working relation, actually is two groups of participants standing pat, reducing their joint effectiveness tremendously. We did not study this relationship.

## 3    Working towards Shared Goals

Shared meaning making is as much an attitude as it is a shared idea about the collaborative activity. It is the attitude of musicians rehearsing a musical piece, building their intersubjective experience from the ground up. It is a form of engagement called empathy: attending to people in their own terms, focusing on eye-contact, gesture, and perhaps in this case, emotion in expression. The associated attitude is what has been called the subjunctive mood: being unassertive, focussing outside oneself, with some restraint in expression, but openness in reception. Described in this way, it appears that meaning making and feelings are interwoven, and the distinction between attitude and process is artificial.

We have discovered that goals of collaboration change during the activity, both at an individual and at group levels. This also applies to feelings. In collaboration, purposes are shared and negotiated, at the beginning, but also during collaboration itself. Indeed, in meaningful collaboration, according to some normative criterion, we may expect feelings about certain ideas to evolve, and be accompanied by evolving feelings that each has for others, as a consequence of sharing and negotiation.

In order to manage emotions during collaboration one needs to have an idea of what good collaboration is (or should be), what its symptoms are, and to what extent the group can handle various emotions by implicit and explicit regulation. This looks like a very general requirement, such as 'be sensitive to what the group needs and know how to react'. However, there is obviously a normative element in what is meant by good collaboration (see Chapter 11 of this book).

The normative dimension of collaboration refers to the application of some principles for the realisation of its goal. One could say this corresponds to a policy, prescribing the objectives of the activity in a particular context. Indeed, it is policies that can define group interactions as collaborative or as something else, for example, as being subjected to party doctrines. Policies can operate on several levels of generality of description. Some general imperative can have great impact on the details: Be brave! Be creative! Respect the other! All religions are equal! Policies can be implicit; in fact, they are constructed as integral to a community in action. For example: informal classroom norms dictate that liking sports is linked to positive emotions, but behaving positively towards the teacher is considered to be less acceptable by the group. This probably applies to boys to a greater extent than to girls.

Communities always have implicit and explicit policies prescribing what counts as appropriate behaviour. This means that every member of the community is supposed to adhere to the policy. Feelings may arise related to what is prescribed as good or bad. This is another reason why collaboration between members of different communities is difficult: people may feel differently about how to behave and what is appropriate.

## 4   Considering Other People in Collaboration

Interaction between people is never neutral. There always is some kind of tension between people, meaning that they are more or less anxious, as revealed by physiological symptoms such as muscle tension, pulse rate, sweating, or pupil dilation. Part of this tension we call relational: it concerns how people feel towards each other, how comfortable they are together, how well they like to work with each other. This tension is greatly affected by two interdependent aspects: the nature of the joint activity and the presence of other people. If the collaborating partners do not feel very competent in the domain, and especially when the activity is open and not well structured, there will be greater sensitivity to relational aspects, involving signals of confirmation or negation of one's actions by others.

In the example shown in the box above, we already noted many of such signs, even though we did not study the facial expressions and gestures of the participants.

Although some people might enjoy being together in leisure activities (e.g. drinking tea), their relationship might become more difficult when they are involved in professional activity (e.g. discussing a new project). When the activity is new, and people feel less secure, more mutual support is beneficial to their collaborative relationship. This does not imply that collaboration should be without tension at all. Indeed, being involved together in some challenging effort requiring full awareness and full use of capabilities will be an activity full of tension. Challenging each other, such as in argumentation, can be a productive experience, whereby partners may increase the depth of understanding what is at stake, making the activity rich with productive tension.

In the example involving administrators and employers, the challenging questions posed by the employer (starting with contribution 2) are indirectly lead to contribution 13, where another participant takes up the previous dialogue as a case in favour of the practical application of open data.

Relational tension is always present during collaborative activities. A main aspect of this tension is the desire to be appreciated by the other, in terms of competence or more vaguely, as a person. This tension can be experienced as negative, when it is restraining collaboration, but also as constructive, when people motivate each other to exert greater effort.

One may wonder in what way the style of question-asking by the employer contributes to such tensions. Perhaps the participants know each other well enough not to be bothered by this. Or, they have learned not to take offense too easily, when this might harm their positions in some virtual hierarchy. It is here that trust in what others may feel could be an important reason for displaying particular emotions clearly or not at all.

But more important for the incentive dimension is that is it satisfying to find out that others have heard you and even understood what you said. Obviously, others may not agree with everything you say; but what is more important is that people react respectfully and benevolently to each other's contributions. This is part of what could be called *ethical consideration*.[7] People must find meaning together in what they are exchanging, whilst preserving, respecting, themselves and others. It is not hard to imagine what happens when people do not respect what others say: we frequently see such things happening in public debates, on television or in personal encounters in daily life. Especially when people ventilate their opinions on political issues on platforms such as Facebook, such contributions can be insulting, personal and even aggressive. Getting used to using and reading such language is not good for mental balance and sensitivity. It only serves to increase negative emotions and to keep people apart, with withdrawal to behaviour and communities where solutions to any issue are nowhere to be found. This has opened up great possibilities for manipulation, by coupling negative feelings to almost any idea or action by the opposing party. Such ideas or actions do not even have to be true.

Conversely, in collaboration, mutual respect seems crucial and requires effort to be managed. The extent to which such management is needed, and with respect to what aspects, depends on many things. For example, quarrelling siblings (collaborating on making fine pastry for their guests) may tolerate many violations of politeness and are able to forgive even rude very personal interventions. In contrast, in a travel agency, whilst collaborating with the client to organise a trip around the world, rudeness from the side of the staff towards the client is inadmissible, and will lead collaboration to a full stop.

## 5   Epilogue

We already noted that the principles of capitalism and hierarchy do not coincide with good collaboration. This is because there often is no equality in purposes of different participants, no shared goals between those who rule and those who are dependent, and no ethical consideration. There also is an issue with freedom of speech. For collaboration this revolves around the question: is one allowed to say everything, to anyone in any situation? The answer should obviously be *no, unless* .... A strong community can tolerate different opinions, and strong collaboration can handle many different views and skills. On the other hand, speech that causes values to conflict undermines equal rights and respect, threatening collaboration, and should in that case be withheld. For the sake of collaboration, we advocate that strong opinions, and the tendency to dominate the discussion with them, are only tolerable when there is both cognitive and ethical consideration, and the group has developed to a sufficient degree of mutual sensitivity and *trust* to tolerate the emotional interaction that may result as a consequence.

But compromising all the time has a price, which is the loss of identity. This is what often happens in politics; due to coalitions with other parties it is hard to discover the principled differences between them. The consequence is that these parties have saved their faces, but are no longer recognised by the public as representing their interests.

Meaning-making is intertwined with many different feelings. Feelings in collaboration concern especially relations to others, and how collaborators react to each other. Many tensions may show up, but the core symptom of collaborators handling emotions well is the development of trust between them. This requires sufficient empathy and the motivation to be considerate.

Development of trust can be a consequence of collaborating over a longer period of time. What develops over time when people work together is what we call *the collaborative working relationship*. This relationship, to say the least, can be characterised by mixed emotions about other participants, especially when they are from other communities that may have different interests and styles of communication. The only way to overcome the negative emotions that may be implied here, is to accept differences and focus on developing sufficient trust to make current collaboration work.

To summarise the normative aspect of collaboration, we think that all behaviour relevant for the development of trust and the tolerance of emotions, characteristic of stable and sensitive relationships, characterises good collaboration. What else may count as 'good' essentially depends on the particular context, e.g. when speed is emphasised, everything contributing to speedy solutions may count as good. In learning contexts, we should be open to all ideas, address them, and understand them. Characterising collaborative relationships, their history and evolution, especially in terms of attitudes and emotions, may be the way to go for further understanding of how participants can regulate productive collaboration.

Finally, if connection is taken as the stronger version of relating, collaboration in music,[8] as we described it in the beginning of this chapter, can be a good example of connecting, as it involves the level of feelings.

### Notes

1 The discussion in this chapter is largely inspired by Baker, Andriessen, and Järvelä (2013).
2 See Bruner (1996, p. 20).
3 See Crook (2013).
4 See Vygotsky (1980).
5 See Wootton (2005).
6 See James (1890, p. 225). The original paraphrase was: "No-one ever had a simple sensation by itself ...".
7 See Allwood, Traum, and Jokinen (2000).
8 See Overy (2012).

### References

Allwood, J., Traum, D., & Jokinen, K. (2000). Cooperation, dialogue and ethics. *International Journal of Human-Computer Studies, 53*(6), 871–914.
Baker, M. J., Andriessen, J., & Järvelä, S. (2013). *Affective learning together: Social and emotional dimensions of collaborative learning.* London: Routledge.

Bruner, J. (1996). *The culture of education*. Cambridge, MA: Harvard University Press.

Crook, C. (2013). Varieties of "togetherness" in learning – And their mediation. In M. Baker, J. Andriessen, & S. Järvelä (Eds.), *Affective learning together: Social and emotional dimensions of collaborative learning* (pp. 41–59). London: Routledge.

James, W. (1890). *The principles of psychology* (Vol. 1). New York, NY: Henry Holt and Company.

Overy, K. (2012). Making music in a group: Synchronization and shared experience. *Annals of the New York Academy of Sciences, 1252*(1), 65–68. https://doi.org/10.1111/j.1749-6632.2012.06530.x

Vygotsky, L. S. (1980). *Mind in society: The development of higher psychological processes*. Cambridge, MA: Harvard University Press.

Wootton, A. J. (2005). *Interaction and the development of mind* (Vol. 15). Cambridge: Cambridge University Press.

CHAPTER 10

# Collaboration and Technology

Human history can be seen from the angle of technological development. As new technologies emerge, they change what people can do, which in turn changes human life.[1] And these changed people invent new technologies: a snowball effect. The obvious examples are fire, flint then bronze and iron tools, writing, printing, railways, electricity, telephones, television, computers, nuclear energy ... and, over the last few decades, the Internet, artificial intelligence, and robots. Although they change human life, technologies can obviously be used for good or bad purposes (however you understand that): fire for cooking or burning at the stake, printing for increased literacy or publishing death warrants, Internet for enabling faster communication and for organising terrorist networks.

There has been talk of economically developed societies living in the Knowledge Age,[2] and now, thanks to social networks, we are supposed to live in the age of collaboration.[3] Of course, the word 'collaboration' has now been largely debased by marketing hype, and all kinds of computer tools, even those that simply enable file sharing, or working the same document over Internet, are described as 'collaborative tools'. Do these kinds of Internet-based tools really enable us to collaborate? If they do, is this a kind of collaboration that we in fact (always) want?

The pros and cons of social media have now been greatly discussed. They can be virtual places of exclusion and alienation just as much as places of more or less genuine friendship. Social media *could* be used for supporting collaboration, as we have defined it so far in this book; but it seems that most often, this is not the case. Collaboration involves thinking of and with the group, working on a shared outcome, with mutual respect. Facebook seems to be mostly a place where people more or less simultaneously and independently shout out what they are doing, blow their own trumpets, assert "look at *me*!" rather than ask "what are *we* doing?".

Consider tools for sharing files, such as dropbox, or tools for writing texts together at a distance, such as googledocs. Is the sharing of files, ones that everyone in the group can look at, 'collaboration'? Of course not; but it could be a useful way of assisting online or offline collaboration, should that be actually engaged in. Neither are googledocs in themselves collaborative, although they could be. Because people could each independently be writing in the common text, without really attending to each other's contributions.

© KONINKLIJKE BRILL NV, LEIDEN, 2020 | DOI: 10.1163/9789004429086_010

Wikipedia is probably the most important tool for 'collective action' via Internet. Anyone who is logged on to Wikipedia has the possibility of typing text into a Wikipedia article, or else to delete it, within constraints of the community's rules. Is Wikipedia a collaborative tool, or a tool for collaboration?

The answer is, of course, yes, collaboration does sometimes happen in Wikipedia, mostly in the discussion pages linked to articles.[4] And this happens mostly when people disagree about the text, which forces them to discuss and try to build a joint solution. Even then, discussion is not necessarily collaborative, basically because with respect to certain contentious topics (such as "The Shroud of Turin", or even "Freud") people simply cannot agree, and do not wish to listen to the other side's point of view. In that case, either the article remains with such a controversy, unfinished, or else it just lists the opposed viewpoints in different sections of the article.[5] But the vast majority of 'contributions' to Wikipedia are isolated people just making some small change to the text, without consulting anyone else. That is not collaboration; it is collective yet independent action on a shared object.

So, Wikipedia is mostly a kind of common 'pot' into which anyone and everyone can throw something, presumably as a function of what is already there. It is a little as if a town organised a 'joint citizens' sculpture' in the main square, beginning with a huge lump of malleable clay and inviting everyone to participate in making the sculpture. It might be made together, but that would require some organisation and collaboration about what the sculpture should be. Or else it could be made by separate individual interventions on the clay, with no-one considering what the others have done: one sculpts an elephant, others cut off the trunk and stick on a trumpet, then someone comes along and paints that red, and so on. This might end up with something interesting(!), but it would not, in this case, be the result of collaboration.

So the point we're making is very simple: such tools *could* be useful for supporting collaboration at a distance, via Internet, but there is *nothing intrinsically collaborative* about these tools: because people could use them either to collaborate or else to each intervene whilst ignoring others.

This relates to the main trajectory that we address in this chapter. As the reader will have understood by now, we have each been around for more than half a century. During the start of our careers, in the 1980s, computers came into the picture as relevant for teaching and learning. Personal computers gradually became affordable, and this was inspiring for many researchers and also for teachers. As researchers, we both spent about half of our lives on studying computers, learning, argumentation and collaboration in educational, but also in professional contexts. We will not summarise all of that work in detail here, but it is striking that our initial enthusiasm about the prospects and our confidence in the possibilities of technology for collaboration has been traumatised. One reason is that we gradually discovered that interacting with technology is socially different from interacting without technology and that this difference has fundamentally been changing our lives. The second reason is related, and it involves simplistic conceptions of working with technology having gradually taken over our lives: control and manipulation. This chapter illustrates our current ambivalence towards technology: we start with an optimistic view, then a depressing section, and end on a positive note.

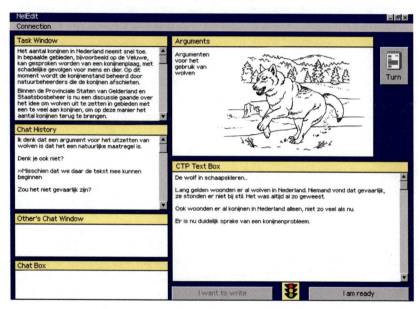

FIGURE 10.1    A tool for writing argumentative texts (developed in the 1990s)

## 1    Collaborative Writing and Technology

I [Jerry] came across a PowerPoint presentation on my computer, called 'The Free University of the Collaborative Future'. It was a proposal for a Summer School that would make the students' learning experiences full of collaboration, on domains called 'Life Span Learning', 'Economy and Psychology', 'Collaboration and Pedagogy', 'Scientific Communities', 'Arguing to Learn', and 'What Europe Means'. It breathes a positive and entrepreneurial spirit, and it dates from only 5 years ago (in 2019). We wanted to engage scholars from various disciplines, many of whom were our friends, in a dialogical and collaborative spirit of working with advanced students. Clearly, there already, we find no mention of technology. We considered technology as obviously integrated in all activities. In the 1980s and 1990s, computers were something exceptional; and people published books with risky titles containing expressions such as 'New Technologies'. But today, information and communication technologies are ubiquitous parts of everyday life for a very large number of persons. Does that also include our collaborative life?

Back to the 1990s: Figure 10.1 shows an example of one of our first collaborative argumentation tools, designed for two students jointly discussing and writing an argumentative text.[6] The tool offered a set of functionalities to the writers supposed to support their text production: a writing tool, a personal notes tool, a tool for chatting, a window with the assignment, and supporting information, such as pictures. Writing is seen as difficult by many, because formulation of coherent ideas into a text that is understood by some audience has to deal with so many constraints at the same time: what to write, how to write it, and how to link it with what is already written.[7] Collaboration might help writers overcoming this complexity. In addition, it may help to provide structure to the complexity of writing, by distinguishing sub-processes of writing, such as planning, idea generation, sentence formulation, linearization, and many others.[8] Technological support for collaborative writing might exploit such subdivision of the writing process, by providing collaborative writers with tools that supported the subtasks of writing. Idea generation could be supported by pictures (as shown in the figure) or lists of prompts, joint planning could benefit from an outline tool, etcetera. At the time, we thought that such technological support for writing a text together would be welcomed by schools.

The collaborative writing tool shown in Figure 10.1 has gradually evolved[9] into a VCRI, the Virtual Collaborative Research Institute[10]: a tool with many more functionalities for working together, including a group awareness tool and a radar diagram for peer feedback. Assessing the contribution of all these components to, for example, good argumentation in a collaborative text, is not an easy task at all. Results about the impact of these and other tools on some characteristics of the writing process and outcomes usually are mixed, which is completely normal for any school assignment. Nevertheless, a survey conducted at the time when these and similar tools for collaborative writing were available in the UK, concluded that their use was nearly absent in British schools.[11] When we look more closely at the results of one of our studies, this could be predicted: there is not much negotiation between the writers at all, most of them simply wanted to write something, anything, they could get away with. They did not want to negotiate, which would entail making their lives harder, just for a school assignment. We thought we had created an assignment affording dialogic inquiry, but what we encountered was all the hurdles that the students still had to conquer before effective dialogic inquiry would be possible.[12] For a learner to move from assignments in which everything is clearly defined to assignments with a lot of freedom, where the difference between right or wrong is insignificant, cannot be achieved by technology alone. What technology did, in this case, and in many other cases, was to make us researchers aware of particular difficulties in the teaching and learning of writing. For this awareness-raising role, technology has given a tremendous boost to almost everything we do.

So, tools can be built for supporting collaboration. Being involved in projects for building web-based environments for various collaborative purposes was, and still is, an important part of our work. We worked, for example, on tools for discussing physics problems,[13] on tools for making argumentative diagrams together,[14] and on tools for creating and working with open data.[15] Designing technology for collaboration is about more than providing functionalities. The next example illustrates the idea that collaboration involves relating to others, and that we need better understanding about how such relating evolves when it is technology-mediated.

## 2    The Collaborative Working Relationship

We assume that in all collaboration, participants evolve in their manifestations of how to work together, in the context of a specific collaborative activity. In normal language: when people work together for a while, they get to know each other as people to work with. This happened when the samurai and the farmers worked together (see Chapter 4): personal and professional relationships evolve during collaborative interaction.

We explained this by introducing the concept of regulation of collaboration.[16] Regulation processes in collaborative learning situations can take two directions: conservative or progressive. In the conservative direction, regulation can be seen as a 'looking-backward' process through which group members reflect on what was right or wrong with their working relationship (social regulation) as well as with the way they shared and negotiated knowledge (cognitive regulation). In the progressive direction, regulation is viewed as a 'looking-forward' process through which collaborators pay attention on how to achieve learning task goals in the future. The way group members regulate their work can be dominated by conservative forces; in such cases, they would be mainly focused on repairing the relation, relegating to a second plane the learning and task goals. It seems that the relationship in such cases is more important than solving the task at hand.

The way group members relate to each other when they use technology is different from how they relate in face-to-face situations. We suppose that this depends on the type of computer-mediated communication, amongst many other things. In some forms of communication, people cannot see each other; they rely on reading text messages. Texting has evolved over the past years, and people have become much better at it, messages revealing emotions, and messages being very concise. We should thereby realise that chat messages often occur in dialogue, with clarification being addressed in follow-up messages.

Interpersonal relations have strong emotional components, group members doing something together may enjoy what they do, but there will always be moments of doubt, tension, hesitation, etc., as we explained in the chapter on emotions (Chapter 9). Such tensions may be different when interaction is mediated through technology. We studied interpersonal tension in a chat environment, where participants were asked to discuss some complicated issue, say genetically modified organisms.[17] As discussed in the chapter on argumentation (Chapter 8), argumentation can be confrontational, especially for personal relationships.[18] We supposed that the way that an opposing statement is formulated relates to the degree that this relationship is under tension. In the same way, tensions could be relaxed with more concessive and sympathetic contributions. This was already established by others, in the context of dinner-table discussions.[19]

As an example, Table 10.1 characterises 6 episodes in a chat-discussion by two girls, Carla and Betty (names changed).

For the actual dialogue, we assessed the amount of tension in the relationship after each utterance, not by recording brain waves, but by relating the formulation of an argumentative statement to the assumed amount of tension. For example, a contribution such as "You are wrong, it should be ..." creates more tension than "You are of course right, but maybe it is a good idea to ...". We compared the tension (and relaxation) with the deepening of argumentation (the number of argumentative statements over time). The graph shown in Figure 10.2 pictures these two measures, on an arbitrary scale from 0–100. It shows the two developments proceed in parallel: more tension (in formulation of statements) accompanies greater depth (adding to a topic with a new aspect) in argumentation, and more relaxation (concession, acknowledgement, etc) relates to less depth (starting a new, unrelated topic), except at the end. Please note this is correlational, we cannot claim which causes what.

COLLABORATION AND TECHNOLOGY 113

TABLE 10.1  Fragment of a chat-discussion between Carla and Betty, on the acceptability of Genetically-Modified Organisms (GMOs)

| Sequence | Dialog extract | Function | Tension/ Relaxation |
|---|---|---|---|
| 1 | Carla: "I'm neither for nor against" | Carla expresses open opinion | Low tension |
| 2 | Carla: "there'll be a better production thus less famine"<br>Betty: "yeah but if it's bad for the organism, then it comes down to the same thing" | Betty demolishes all of Carla's arguments | Higher tension |
| 3 | Carla: "but tell me i think you're against so explain why to me will you?"<br>Betty: "because it's bad for the human organisms"<br>…<br>Betty: "yeah sure maybe we'll even be cloned"<br>Carla: "yes it's true but ya know i am totally against cloning any individual" | Betty argues against, and Carla concedes | Lower tension |
| 4 | Carla: "why are you against GMOs? Isn't there a single positive argument in your opinion?"<br>Betty: "phhh maybe but nothing has been proved, for the vaccinations nothing has been proved." | Betty asks Carla to clarify her ideas, but Betty refuses | Higher tension |
| 5 | Carla: "every solution begins from hypotheses so why are you closing yourself up in this opinion??????"<br>…<br>Betty: "i'm telling you that if man starts with the plants, after they going to want to do more and it's going to degenerate and soon we ourselves are going to be genetically modified and after it'll get worse as time goes on …"<br>Carla: "in the medical domain, in the environment, public health, food, economy<br>but I completely agree with you" | Carla challenges Betty's reasonableness but has to concede again | Higher tension |
| 6 | Carla: "c'mon now we have to resume our discussion"<br>Betty: "for the environment and for food, i would really be surprised<br>the synthesis is that you are for and i'm against" | Change of focus, summary statements | Lower tension |

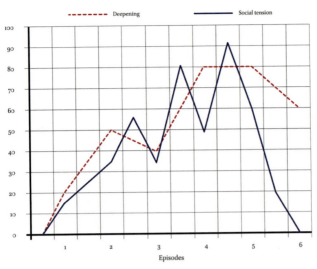

FIGURE 10.2  A graph depicting deepening of a debate and the relational tensions over time (6 episodes)

In a good collaborative relationship, the participants know how to deal with tensions, handling them according to their moment-by-moment estimate of what the relationship and the goals of the assignment require. Our exploratory work can therefore be seen as a concrete illustration of the inseparability of relational and cognitive dimensions of interactions between persons, even, or maybe especially, in technology mediated interactions.

Clearly, the expression of the interpersonal relationship in the interaction between the two girls is influenced by the technology. For example, all of the interpersonal communication must go through the typewritten modality, which, although slowing down the interaction, can form a permanent trace (on the screen) for shared reflection.[20] Moreover, communication of affect by facial expression and gesture is excluded. Despite the experience of young persons over time in adapting to some of these shortcomings, expression of affect may nevertheless lack subtility.

## 3   Collaboration and Technology in Professional Life

In real life contexts, predicting exactly how technology will actually be used is often difficult. This can be a problem in the context of cybercrime: attempts to steal our identities, our money, or simply to frustrate our work by infecting our computers, rely on exceptions, derogations, people not paying attention, or not understanding what is at stake. There are various ways for the criminal mind to operate, but our concern is that collaboration can be a better way for

# COLLABORATION AND TECHNOLOGY

users to deal with cybercrime than upholding strict regulations. That reality is different, as we will describe with the following analysis of missed opportunities for collaboration in a study about how users experienced cybercrime at their workplace. We undertook this study at the administration of a municipality (200 000 inhabitants) in a country in Europe. For reasons of privacy, we will not reveal the name of the project in which this study was undertaken.

For understanding the role of cybersecurity within the organisation, we organised a story-telling workshop.[21] We think stories are a good way to capture personal experiences. However, in our workshop, we added the collaborative dimension. In our view, a collaborative story (a story that is written together) can be taken as a joint understanding by the participants and a coherent integration of their personal experiences. The story-telling workshop that we organised involved small groups of participants from the municipality (system administrators and users from various departments) in collaborative efforts to produce meaningful stories about their cybersecurity experiences. We first asked individual participants to think about an event of their personal experience related to cybersecurity. We then asked them to form small groups (3–5 people) to collaboratively broaden and deepen[22] elements of the story according to a number of topics: the organisation, the system, precise actions undertaken, their emotions and the resulting perspective on cybersecurity in their municipality. Figure 10.3 represents the relation between the characteristic elements of a story (orientation, complication and resolution) and the underlying broadening and deepening as an iceberg model.[23] The collaborative phase lasted about half an hour for each story. The plenary presentation of the first four stories took about 90 minutes, as the presentations invoked a lot of discussion. We collected 6 stories in total, this process lasting a full morning.

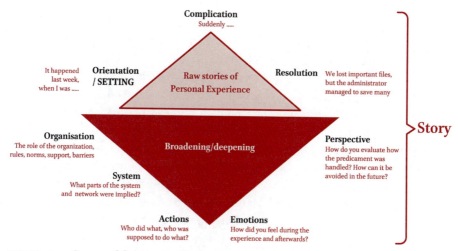

FIGURE 10.3   Our use of the story to collect experiences with cybercrime

An example of a typical story is the following:

> One of the tasks of this employee (E) is to read all mail the mayor receives, which may comprise several hundreds of emails every day. In spite of strict regulations, E opened an infected email. This mail had no subject, which could have caused suspicion. After E opened the mail, files in each directory on his computer he accessed became inaccessible. The IT-Department was notified, they discovered a type of ransomware that had encrypted all the files in the directories E had accessed. The computer was restored in the IT-Department, where all files that were not yet accessed were retrieved, and the system was reinstalled, and the intact files were restored. Infected files could not be retrieved. E was initially terrified, feared the computer was lost, but now sees this as a lesson learned, to more strictly apply the rules in such cases.

From the viewpoint of collaboration, we can imagine users collaborating on a) detection and understanding of an issue; b) deciding what to do; c) informing other users of what happened. This could be done formally (by following regulations) or informally, or both. Also, we could expect collaboration between the IT-department and individual users, as well as with the user community (other users in the organisation) on sharing a particular incident, and on explaining and adapting regulations for prevention of cyberincidents. The IT-department is expected to make logs of incidents, consult with other departments about specific incidents and how to deal with them, and to share cybersecurity issues with management and security authorities. What we call collaboration here is more than discussion. The main reason we call for collaboration is because we insist on considering the other in this activity, as equals, as being in the same boat, and on envisaging a joint goal of combatting cybercrime. This is an attitude as much as it is a vision on how to act. We did not find such an attitude, nor a vision, although the stories do reveal a cooperative and positive climate. We only discuss the user activities here.

Our analysis starts from the views of users in their organisations, not from the nature of the technological issue. Therefore, we need a framework that does justice to the organisation in which the user is working, and how that relates to how a user experiences the technological issues, including their resolution. We consider the user with an issue to be addressed as part of an *activity system*. An activity is seen as a system of human 'doing' whereby a subject works on an object in order to obtain a desired outcome. In order to do this, the subject employs tools, which may be physical (e.g. an axe, a computer) or semiotic (e.g. a plan, a text). An activity system further pictures an individual as part of a system characterised by particular rules, communities and division of labour.[24] An activity is a hierarchical structure, and its nature changes over time.[25] This change can be related to tensions in the system, so tensions can be a good thing.

Figure 10.4 shows the activity system for users with cybersecurity issues in this municipality. First, there is a *subject*, which is the generic user of techno-services who has the *objective* of making use of a computer (the tool) as a regular part of the job, but is faced with some obstacle so that the regular activity cannot be performed. This is the initial issue, and it gives rise to a shifted objective: the resolution of the technical issue. Characteristically, this user does not have the knowledge (*tools*) to resolve the issue, for which the user needs the IT-department.

The subject is part of the *community* of all other users within a department. These users frequently interact, but we do not know the extent to which these interactions concern cybersecurity. The small number of stories that we collected show that our users may have some awareness of risks, but there is no general (formal) procedure for sharing cybersecurity issues with all members of the community, or within a particular department.

What users are all supposed to share is the rules: there is a clear set of safety-regulations set out by the IT-Department for secure cyber behaviour. The most important one is: "all *users* are warned not to open e-mails from unknown senders or without a subject or with attached files in .zip or .exe format".

The *division of labour* is very clear: all cyber issues will be handled by the IT-Department. They are seen as competent, reliable, quick, especially good at estimating the risk for the organisation and at taking the necessary measures. On the other hand, our users know that they themselves are seen by the IT-Department as risks, possible sources of mistakes, who need to stick to the regulations to avoid making these mistakes.

This leads to the final part of the activity system, which is the *tool*. The user, any user, probably understands how to operate the computer as an instrument for doing some jobs. As a tool, it functions in so far it is needed. Part of the meaning of the tool is doing the job correctly. If this fails, then the machine is not a tool anymore, but an obstacle.

At first sight, one might locate the main source of *tension* in technology: a system, or computer that has an issue. In our analysis, the tension also is sought in the underlying components of the organisational activity system: the rules, the division of labour and the community. This means that the main source of tension is not just a *malfunction* of the technology, it is the fact that *users experience opaqueness of security issues*: generally, users do not understand the nature of the problem, and therefore rely on the expertise of the IT-Department for resolution, but also for awareness about causes and the severity of the threat. This probably applies to most users of technology in other contexts – we do not assume that this is specific to our current group of participants.

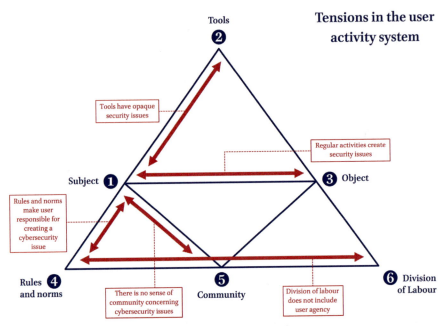

FIGURE 10.4  Tensions (red arrows) between components in the user activity system

More specifically for our users is the fact that tension can be caused because their *regular user activities may create security issues*, meaning for example that it can be in the job description of some employees that they have to open all emails, or that they have to sometimes work with files from external sources. These first two types of potential tension are quite general, and will always be there.

Three more fundamental potential sources of tension relate to how cybersecurity issues are dealt with in the organisation. The main potential source of tension of a service-user is that whilst these users assume responsibility for mistakes, the division of labour is such that *users experience no agency in dealing with cybersecurity issues,* so their learning is limited. They are merely reminded of adhering to the rules, and as a consequence *they experience guilt for having the issue*. Moreover, there is a transparency issue: *the community (of other users in the municipality) remains uninformed* about issues and potential dangers. Actually, in cybersecurity, there is no notion of community of users at all.

We need to stress that the stories showed strong points and assets in the organisation as well. The stories reveal that the IT-Department was very easy to reach, always ready to help, involved competent people as individuals, and also as a team, and seemed very efficient in doing their job. Their organisation seemed very adequate and internal lines of communication were short, with frequent (informal) communication between its members. We do not further discuss the IT-Department activity system here.

This very brief analysis of how people deal with cybersecurity issues within a medium-large municipality, based on a limited set of user stories, serves to illustrate a number of important points, that relate to our understanding of technology use and collaboration in professional contexts.

First, in addition to building technology for collaboration, as we saw in the section on collaborative writing, there is also, in many professional contexts, a need for building collaboration for technology. This could be about how to deal with technology and its various issues. Especially urgent, we believe, is the need to collaborate to fight cybercrime.

Second, in addition to looking at tensions at the level of interactions between people, we can also look at tensions at the level of activity systems. The first level of analysis addresses relations between individuals. It seems that this second level of analysis addresses quite well how people deal with technology, and explains that there is not enough collaboration.

Third, technology impacts both levels of interaction. It affects relations between people and the possibilities for handling these. It also affects the nature of the issues that people in organisations have to handle. In both, collaboration is affected. Also, collaboration could be a facilitating force, as would be the case when professionals view cybersecurity as a shared issue threatening everybody equally, only to be solved by joining forces, including with others outside of the department, to understand and fight attacks. As long as cybercrime is considered to be an individual issue to be repaired, it will continue to exist and to grow in strength.

## 4   Bypassing Collaboration

In addition to the thumbs up and down discourse in social media, there is the algorithm, currently developed and exploited by commercial companies as well as public organisations to control our behaviour or to make money from it. Algorithms have started ruling our lives: what advertisements we see on Facebook, who will be released from prison, what we pay for our health insurance. Our lives will be following the laws and simplifications of computers, or what they can put into their algorithms. To build an algorithm you need data about what happened in the past, and you need clear definitions of success. The algorithm looks for data associated with success; it learns what data are the best associates. This association is correlational, it relates coincidental phenomena (clicking on a nice car advert, liking a comment about the American president), and it is not interested in explanations (e.g. why would these two behaviours actually be related?). Moreover, the success criteria (what is defined as success) are not necessarily those that relate to greater quality of our lives, but rather to maximising profit for the company under whose instigation the algorithm was developed. Algorithms therefore are opinions embedded in code. Third, the collected data and the resulting algorithms represent past practices, hence the biases of past practices, in our wonderful imperfect world.[26] For example, algorithms might predict that the next crime will occur in a poor neighbourhood, performed by a high-risk individual. Those high-risk individuals will most likely not be people of Caucasian ethnicity with jobs, wives, husbands and children. Finally, we are building some kind of system about things we do not really understand. These systems are black boxes: it is rarely revealed on what data and criteria an algorithm works; it does not tell us its foundational principles and the data it is based on – because we are dealing with opinions rather than facts. And we may not agree with these opinions at all. Algorithms should be transparent. We cannot outsource our responsibilities to data scientists and efficiency or profit-oriented ideas of success: we must consider human values and human ethics underlying these algorithms.[27]

So, how about an algorithm for collaboration? Can we define what success looks like, and can we tell on what data this algorithm should be based? This calls for serious research, not for correlations. During the time that researchers studied computer-mediated interaction to design support for that interaction, algorithms were developed that replace that interaction, making interaction an obsolete phenomenon.

## 5    Online Media Promoting Collaboration

There is a great risk that current technology will deskill interaction, and therefore collaboration. Technology has changed the way we interact, or more precisely, the meaning we assign to interaction: when, how and about what we interact with others. To what extent can technologies support collaboration? In our terms, can technologies support working together as equals, shared meaning making and with mutual respect?

Consider the example of a recent project, carried out by Jerry and colleagues involving young children (4 and 5 year olds) sharing photos and films, using an application enabling collection and display on a whiteboard. The photos showed scenes from the children's private lives, such as their breakfasts. The teacher projected the display on a whiteboard in the classroom. The context of the activity was a project about dealing with diversity in multi-ethnic classrooms.

Maybe it is good to freeze the following scene (see Figure 10.5): a classroom with a large whiteboard in the centre of the wall, and a small group of children looking at the photos. The teacher is standing next to the whiteboard. The whiteboard displays the collection of individual photos of all children with their breakfast, all photos together on the same display. The breakfasts may look different, but what is experienced here, whether intended or not, is *equality*. All children are represented by their photos, and all photos are there showing breakfast. It is not about individuals showing off, it is about all children sharing a similar aspect of their lives. The difference between the showing off and sharing is delicate, but here it is crucial. The display could serve as a basis for further developing a sense of equality, also in multi-ethnic classrooms. This equality can be a basis for developing mutual respect and curiosity, through collaborative activity.

FIGURE 10.5   Kids sharing pictures of their breakfast displayed on a digiboard (drawing by Roxane Oudart-Détienne)

Could the teacher have used Facebook, or Google Photo, or something else? Yes, she could have. But those platforms do not afford our trust in equality and consideration, as we do not know how they handle our privacy. Also, inviting the kids to like or dislike the photos would have immediately reduced the meaning of their interactions. This would have enhanced differences rather than leading them to embrace them.

Could the teacher have used different technology, such as paper and tape, displaying all pictures on a large poster? That could have happened as well, even as a collaborative activity. But then there would be a subtle difference, the pictures would have been manipulated and discussed before they were displayed, which would probably lead the kids to discussing differences rather than promoting the sense of equality. The teacher could have created the poster on her own, displaying it on the wall in front of the class. It would be harder to do, but perhaps with the same impact.

Before the advent of Facebook and the like, online communities already existed. Some were highly social and collaborative; these were the reasons for their existence.[28] There are online gaming communities that are very collaborative too.[29] The point we are making is this: technology can reinforce existing processes, cause modification of them, as well as create new possibilities. But this may go in all directions, creating new meaning for interaction and collaboration, often bypassing our lack of understanding. The powers that are at work in society are not the powers that necessarily favour collaboration.

## 6 Conclusion: Collaboration and Technology

As researchers, we have participated in many projects in which technology was developed to support collaborative discussion, argumentation, or other forms of co-creation, affording sharing with people elsewhere, potentially covering many physical distances between participants. Notwithstanding many positive aspects of such technology for collaboration we would like to point out, in conclusion, three aspects that made us a bit wary about using technology.

First, using technology transforms both interpersonal and organisational interaction. Even the simplest chat tool has given a lot of people the opportunity to engage in different types of interactions. Many aggressive discussions on chat forums exemplify one of such types. New opportunities for interactions are created by technology but it has turned out to be difficult for technology to create constructive interactions. It is quite hard to create situations of positive interdependence,[30] in which constructive use of technology is actually possible.

The second issue is that our participations on various Internet platforms have been and probably are misused. Not by the paparazzi, but by people with the unethical desires of making money and influencing decision-making in society. The same will happen with the Internet of things: for example, intelligent homes that tell our energy company how we live, or intelligent television telling Netflix what we are watching. One the one hand, we would like solutions in (for example) health or education based on knowledge about individuals, for example that a record is kept about our history. On the other hand, we do not like details of our history to become available to commercial companies or other organisations that are not transparent about how they use this information. More transparency is a prerequisite for ethical consideration of human needs: otherwise, a lack of trust will evolve instead of compliance.

Finally, instead of discovering what works and why, simplified solutions are ruling what people do. Algorithms decide about our insurance, our bank loans, and our being good citizens. Technology in education has been taken over by commercial companies too. Although most of our interactions and collaborations involve refined relational mutual understanding, algorithm-based technology treats these as gross correlational coincidences we do not need to understand at all. Such simplifications lead to simple reasoning, and simple people. This is the opposite of what we would like to see from the viewpoint of collaboration: technology affording considerate solutions, including the collective long-term needs of communities rather than those of money-makers.

**Notes**

1   See Säljö (2004).
2   See Bereiter (2005).
3   See Dyer (2010). Also have a look at https://www.theguardian.com/optus-business-smart-future/2016/oct/05/the-age-of-collaboration?CMP=share_btn_link
4   See Détienne, Baker, Fréard, Barcellini, Denis, and Quignard (2016).
5   See Baker, Détienne, and Barcellini (2017).
6   See Andriessen, Erkens, Van De Laak, Peters, and Coirier (2003).
7   See Bereiter and Scardamalia (1989).
8   See Coirier, Andriessen, and Chanquoy (1999).
9   See Phielix, Prins, Kirschner, Erkens, and Jaspers (2011).
10  See Jaspers, Broeken, and Erkens (2004).
11  See Crook et al. (2008).
12  See Renshaw and van der Linden (2004).
13  See de Vries, Lund, and Baker (2002).
14  See Belgiorno, De Chiara, Manno, Overdijk, Scarano, and van Diggelen (2008).
15  See Scarano et al. (2017).

16 See van der Puil, Andriessen, and Kanselaar (2004).
17 See Andriessen, Baker, and van der Puil (2010).
18 See Bales (1950).
19 See Muntigl and Turnbull (1998).
20 See Clark and Brennan (1991).
21 See Kurtz (2014). Also have a look at http://cognitive-edge.com/blog/category/narrative/
22 See Baker, Andriessen, Lund, van Amelsvoort, and Quignard (2007).
23 See Labov and Waletzky (1997).
24 See Engeström, Miettinen, and Punamäki (1999).
25 See Leont'ev (1974).
26 See O'Neil (2017). See also https://www.ted.com/talks/cathy_o_neil_the_era_of_blind_faith_in_big_data_must_end
27 See Tufekci (2017). See also https://www.ted.com/talks/zeynep_tufekci_machine_intelligence_makes_human_morals_more_important and https://www.ted.com/talks/zeynep_tufekci_we_re_building_a_dystopia_just_to_make_people_click_on_ads
28 See Rheingold (2008).
29 See Gui (2018).
30 See Sharples et al. (2016).

## References

Andriessen, J., Baker, M., & van der Puil, C. (2010). Socio-cognitive tensions in collaborative working relations. In S. Ludvigsen, A. Lund, I. Rasmussen, & R. Säljö (Eds.), *Learning across sites: New tools, infrastructures and practices* (pp. 222–242). London: Pergamon Press.

Andriessen, J., Erkens, G., Van De Laak, C., Peters, N., & Coirier, P. (2003). Argumentation as negotiation in electronic collaborative writing. In J. Andriessen, M. Baker, & D. Suthers (Eds.), *Arguing to learn* (pp. 79–115). Dordrecht: Springer.

Baker, M., Andriessen, J., Lund, K., van Amelsvoort, M., & Quignard, M. (2007). Rainbow: A framework for analysing computer-mediated pedagogical debates. *International Journal of Computer-Supported Collaborative Learning, 2*(2–3), 315–357. https://doi.org/10.1007/s11412-007-9022-4

Baker, M. J., Détienne, F., & Barcellini, F. (2017). Argumentation and conflict management in online epistemic communities: A narrative approach to Wikipedia debates. In F. Arcidiacono & A. Bova (Eds.), *Interpersonal argumentation in educational and professional contexts* (pp. 141–157). Cham: Springer.

Bales, R. F. (1950). A set of categories for the analysis of small group interaction. *American Sociological Review, 15*, 257–263.

Belgiorno, F., De Chiara, R., Manno, I., Overdijk, M., Scarano, V., & van Diggelen, W. (2008). Face to face cooperation with CoFFEE. In P. Dillenbourg & M. Specht (Eds.), *Times of convergence. Technologies across learning contexts* (Vol. 5192, pp. 49–57). https://doi.org/10.1007/978-3-540-87605-2_6

Bereiter, C. (2005). *Education and mind in the knowledge age*. London: Routledge.

Bereiter, C., & Scardamalia, M. (1989). *The psychology of written composition*. London: Routledge.

Clark, H. H., & Brennan, S. E. (1991). Grounding in communication. In L. B. Resnick, L. M. Levine, & S. D. Teasley (Eds.), *Perspectives on socially shared cognition* (pp. 127–149). Washington, DC: APA.

Coirier, P., Andriessen, J., & Chanquoy, L. (1999). From planning to translating: The specificity of argumentative writing. In J. Andriessen & P. Coirier (Eds.), *Foundations of argumentative text processing* (pp. 1–28). Amsterdam: University of Amsterdam Press.

Crook, C., Fisher, T., Graber, R., Harrison, C., Lewin, C., Cummings, J., ... Sharples, M. (2008). *Implementing Web 2.0 in secondary schools: Impacts, barriers and issues*. Coventry: Becta.

Détienne, F., Baker, M., Fréard, D., Barcellini, F., Denis, A., & Quignard, M. (2016). The descent of Pluto: Interactive dynamics, specialisation and reciprocity of roles in a Wikipedia debate. *International Journal of Human-Computer Studies, 86*, 11–31. https://doi.org/10.1016/j.ijhcs.2015.09.002

de Vries, E., Lund, K., & Baker, M. (2002). Computer-mediated epistemic dialogue: Explanation and argumentation as vehicles for understanding scientific notions. *Journal of the Learning Sciences, 11*(1), 63–103. https://doi.org/10.1207/S15327809JLS1101_3

Dyer, K. (2010). Challenges of maintaining academic integrity in an age of collaboration, sharing and social networking. In *TCC Worldwide Online Conference* (pp. 168–195). Hawaii, HI: TCC.

Engeström, Y., Miettinen, R., & Punamäki, R.-L. (1999). *Perspectives on activity theory*. Cambridge: Cambridge University Press.

Gui, D. A. F. (2018). Virtual sense of community in a world of warcraft® storytelling open forum thread. *Journal of Virtual Worlds Research, 11*(2), 1–17.

Jaspers, J., Broeken, M., & Erkens, G. (2004). *Virtual Collaborative Research Institute (VCRI)* (Version 2.0). Utrecht: Onderwijskunde Utrecht, ICO/ISOR.

Kurtz, C. (2014). *Working with stories in your community or organization: Participatory narrative inquiry* (3rd ed.). New York, NY: Kurtz-Fernhout Publishing.

Labov, W., & Waletzky, J. (1997). Narrative analysis: Oral versions of personal experience. *Journal of Narrative & Life History, 7*(1–4), 3–38. http://dx.doi.org/10.1075/jnlh.7.02nar

Leont'ev, A. N. (1974). The problem of activity in psychology. *Soviet Psychology, 13*(2), 4–33.

Muntigl, P., & Turnbull, W. (1998). Conversational structure and facework in arguing. *Journal of Pragmatics, 29*, 225–256. https://doi.org/10.1016/S0378-2166(97)00048-9

O'Neil, C. (2017). *Weapons of math destruction: How big data increases inequality and threatens democracy*. New York, NY: Broadway Books.

Phielix, C., Prins, F. J., Kirschner, P. A., Erkens, G., & Jaspers, J. (2011). Group awareness of social and cognitive performance in a CSCL environment: Effects of a peer feedback and reflection tool. *Computers in Human Behavior, 27*(3), 1087–1102.

Renshaw, P., & van der Linden, J. (2004). Curriculum as dialogue. In J. Terwel & D. Walker (Eds.), *Curriculum as a shaping force: Toward a principled approach in curriculum theory and practice* (pp. 17–32). New York, NY: Nova Science Publishers.

Rheingold, H. (2008). Virtual communities – Exchanging ideas through computer bulletin boards. *Journal of Virtual Worlds Research, 1*(1), 1–5.

Säljö, R. (2004). Learning and technologies, people and tools in co-ordinated activities. *International Journal of Educational Research, 41*(6), 489–494. https://doi.org/10.1016/j.ijer.2005.08.013

Scarano, V., Malandrino, D., Baker, M., Détienne, F., Andriessen, J., Pardijs, M., ... Ruijer, E. (2017). Fostering citizens' participation and transparency with social tools and personalization. In A. Ojo & J. Millard (Eds.), *Public administration and information technology. Government 3.0 – Next generation government technology infrastructure and services* (pp. 197–218). https://doi.org/10.1007/978-3-319-63743-3_8

Sharples, M., de Roock, R., Ferguson, R., Gaved, M., Herodotou, C., Koh, E., ... Wong, L. H. (2016). *Innovating Pedagogy 2016: Exploring new forms of teaching, learning and assessment, to guide educators and policy makers*. Innovation report 5, Institute of Educational Technology, The Open University.

Snowden, D. (2005). From atomism to networks in social systems. *The Learning Organization, 12*(6), 552.

Tufekci, Z. (2017). *Twitter and tear gas: The power and fragility of networked protest*. New Haven, CT: Yale University Press.

van der Puil, C., Andriessen, J., & Kanselaar, G. (2004). Exploring relational regulation in computer-mediated (collaborative) learning interaction: A developmental perspective. *CyberPsychology & Behavior, 7*(2), 183–195.

CHAPTER 11

# The Principles of Collaboration (How to Do It)

If you have got this far in this book, you will know something about its authors. We are not the kind of people who impose strict rules or who provide simple recipes for how to deal with complex social issues. This chapter will therefore be about general considerations on doing collaboration, about being flexible, reflexive and having the right spirit in a complex world.

A number of researchers have proposed rules for working together in an effective way. Two British educational researchers, Neil Mercer and Rupert Wegerif, have defined rules for what they call both 'thinking together' and 'productive discussion' in educational situations. They include letting everyone speak, listening, being positive, raising questions, respecting others, challenging if one does not agree, sticking to the topic and being ready to compromise.[1] Other researchers, working on collaborative problem-solving[2] and collaborative design,[3] have defined a number of 'dimensions' of group activity, along which it can be evaluated, such as the division of labour between working on the task and working on the group, the degree of mutual understanding, the extent to which conflicts are resolved cooperatively, and so on.

These rules and dimensions make sense, and it has been shown that teaching them has positive effects. However, remembering them in the heat of the action may well be quite hard. We think that they are all covered by the three principles described in chapter one of this book. They can be summed up in three keywords: *equality*, *co-construction* and *mutual respect*. Let us look at each in turn.

*Equality*. Consider others as having valuable things to contribute just as much as yourself. Think about the balance of your joint work, and whether all are having their fair say about the matter. If it looks unequal, invite some more retiring people to contribute. Of course, do not try to dominate the collaboration, even if you think you are smarter than the others, because if you want to speak alone, you don't need others.

*Co-construction*. This means not only generating ideas but – above all – constructing them in terms of the ideas expressed by the *others* with whom you are collaborating. That is co-construction. Being co-constructive also means dealing with conflict, disagreement, in certain ways that were discussed in Chapter 8 of this book. Do not try to enforce your own view: try to see the other's point of view, call yourself into question, and try to raise up above the discussion to find a new way of seeing things, acceptable to all, that would *dissolve*, rather than *resolve*, conflicts.

*Mutual respect.* We would not advise collaboration between people who do not respect each other. We mean respect for other people's ideas, even if you do not agree with them, at least at first. And respect for others as people. It is not acceptable to totally ignore the feelings of others. Of course, not all ideas and people *should* be respected, notably ideas that, basically, are based on lack of respect and on discrimination. You cannot collaborate with such people. In sum, choose carefully the people you collaborate with; make sure they respect the three criteria of collaboration and that you are also able to do so with them. Finally, be flexible in applying these guidelines, paying attention to the context in which you are collaborating.

### Notes

1. This is a summary of different versions of these rules, present in a large number of publications, extensive references to which can be found on the Cambridge University 'thinking together' website: http://thinkingtogether.educ.cam.ac.uk/publications/
2. See Meier, Spada, and Rummel (2007).
3. See Détienne, Baker, and Burkhardt (2012).

### References

Détienne, F., Baker, M., & Burkhardt, J.-M. (2012). Quality of collaboration in design meetings: Methodological reflexions. *CoDesign: International Journal of CoCreation in Design, 8*(4), 247–261.

Meier, A., Spada, H., & Rummel, N. (2007). A rating scheme for assessing the quality of computer-supported collaboration processes. *International Journal of Computer Supported Collaborative Learning, 2*(1), 63–86. https://doi.org/10.1007/s11412-006-9005-x

CHAPTER 12

# Collaboration: The Warp and Weft of Society

## 1     A Participatory View on Society

In this chapter, we will explore the extent to which collaboration has a place in institutionalised practices, with their underlying ideologies.

People are not free-floating entities. In Chapter 7 of this book on learning we looked at individual learners as participants in structures of on-going social practices.[1] This view on learning (there are others) looks at the subjective experience of individuals in social practices. A social practice, which can be defined as the customary behaviours of people participating in habitually occurring meaningful activity (*normal* people in *normal* contexts), is the context of interactions between people. This participation is crucial to the quality of relationships, understandings, orientations, feelings and thoughts. If we want to understand people, we need to look at how they participate in their social practices, such as with their friends, in their homes, in their workplaces. People's participation has an impact on the social practice, and that practice influences how people behave; so a person's participation is only partially personal. People learn to do things in the process of participating with others. Learning to do things does not come only from books or from explanation from others; it comes primordially from participation with other people during (sometimes) collaborative action. Books, instruction, demonstration, may support reflection, but it is the actual doing which leads to the meaning-making. As we have stated and reiterated in this book, collaboration is a type of participation characterised by equality, co-construction and mutual respect.

Currently, in comparison with times before the Internet, physical places and social practices are greatly interlinked, and a practice is not necessarily confined to a single location. People are moving around in various places and practices, and particular practices can be understood as partaking in more comprehensive ones. Local practices are related to the overall structure of practices (let us call this *society*) in various ways, characterising what overall influences make a difference on a local practice and how a local practice can have an impact on the overall structure. People behave differently in different practices: they need to interpret and appropriate standards and rules of a practice to be good participants. Their modes of pursuing their interests across contexts are not the same. Their involvements in practices, and with issues within these practices will not be the same, and will often be only partial.

Practices are messy, not homogeneous. Society is not something designed by people according to some cunning masterplan: there is a mix of constructive and destructive powers operating all the time, having different impacts on practices as well as on individual participants.

Biological and anthropological studies tell us that collaboration is a natural survival mechanism for humans, but also for primates and even other species. There exists a natural interdependency between people; if they do not participate appropriately, they will become extinct. This applies to every species: even ants act together in order to survive.[2] Within the view we are expounding, *society can be defined as what has been accomplished by collaboration*,[3] as society has evolved, in a positive sense, from people acting together respectfully for meaningful purposes. If collaboration suffers, society will decline.[4] Collaboration may suffer when there is insufficient equality, when some have more power than others, which is linked to more wealth and influence. Collaboration greatly suffers when there is a lack of shared understanding of values about what is important in society, and what we all hold as being true and important. In the view of David Bohm,[5] shared understanding (established by collaboration) is the cement of our society. Collaboration may suffer from lack of mutual respect.

If shared understanding is the cement, equality is the structure of society, setting the standard for what is generally permissible and supported. Mutual respect sets the pragmatic rules for refined (or less refined) forms of interaction, through which our collaborative meaning-making evolves. Obviously, there are practices that do not involve full equality, and we all know examples of individuals or groups of individuals who act according to their private interests (power and money) even though other people will have to pay and suffer for it. As we are writing this, there is a lot to say for the claim that society is crumbling down. Large organisations with the sole ambition of scraping all the money they can get from those who are less fortunate are exercising legitimate power in many societies.[6] Please realise there were times when an Eskimo who had become very rich would hold a giant feast in which he divided up his possessions among those in his tribe.[7] It might be that what we are currently witnessing (or participating in), at least in the western world, is the end of the individualistic society as we know it. The collaborative society may then be coming, as alternative collaborative practices already are emerging.[8]

Or is it? It would perhaps be a good idea to have a closer look at what we mean by such a society and what the other side of collaboration is like. On one hand, people can be remarkably collaborative, and there are biological and cultural reasons for positing the existence of universal mechanisms of cultural group selection: survival of the groups with cultural advantages, such as customs and traditions.[9] On the other hand, we see individual interest being pursued on an unprecedented scale, and we seem to be heading for great environmental disaster. This is not 'natural'[10]; but what can we say about collaboration here?

## 2   De-Skilling Collaboration

How is modern society deskilling collaboration?[11] First, as we have seen, collaboration requires equality and current society is characterised by increasing inequality. Metaphorically speaking, there are winners, farmers and heroes and bandits, and they are not recognised as equals. Few are extremely rich; many do not have anything. Second, there is a focus on individualistic activities, for example, individuals rather than teams are rewarded for their performance. Except for some team activities, in which collaboration can be recognised, at least by experts (recall the football team: who in the audience is able to understand collaboration in football, in addition to individual technical skills or individuals scoring goals?), it is much easier to evaluate individual performance. For example, individual scientists are evaluated by the number of articles that they have published in highly-rated scientific journals. Although much scientific work at universities is, or should be, collaborative, only individuals are promoted and their output evaluated.[12] Recall the Samurai example (Chapter 4): how did they perform as a team? Do you recall individual efforts or team efforts? Third, we have learned that development of collaboration takes time and requires a mind-set, before trust is strong enough. The farmers and Samurai did not trust each other at the beginning; only the wise men understood that trust needed time to evolve. Farmers and samurai had several weeks of being together for that to evolve. Some bonding activities may have helped. In current society, projects last only a limited amount of time, and collaborative assignments are usually short-lived. In such a setting, collaboration does not get sufficient time to evolve, let alone to become institutionalised into practices. Fourth, in professional contexts, specialised work is carried out in isolation from other specialised work. This is called the silo effect[13]: people work inside their own office spaces and hardly meet people from other office spaces and specialisations. The farmers keep on farming, and only interact with the samurai under very special circumstances. Often, people are not even aware that these other specialisations exist, or what the people next door are working on. Instead of realising that there may be dependencies between various specialisations, and that sustainability of collaborative dependencies inside a system need to be managed,[14] new workers and managers need to reinvent their wheels and tools every time. Without collaboration, knowledge gets lost, or remains with a few specialists until they fade away. And finally, we are facing the tendency of ignoring emotions and striving for complete homogenization of behaviour in society. This is the principle of *conditional equality*; all people are equal, if they conform to the main culture, otherwise they are considered a problem. All behaviour should be rational, and we should not display emotions, unless they are positive and constructive.[15] This interpretation of equality without respect turns into the opposite of the idea of collaboration. Turning concepts into their opposites to suit the needs of opportunistic reasoning, instead of looking at sustainability of what has been achieved, is the fate of any artificial construction of thought.

One of the areas where this lack of equality and respect is made especially manifest is education. Just like anyone, teachers are not only either good or bad.[16] Just like everyone, teachers as individuals have certain qualities that make them good professionals, but they may also lack some of them. Demands are changing all the time. To make students listen, or at least to pay attention, requires knowing what you are doing. It does not suffice to say that a teacher should be interesting, if not captivating, or be a charismatic personality. Many teachers are only moderately interesting, and not very charismatic but may still be good teachers. They might be particularly knowledgeable, or experienced, or understand their students very well. It always is a mix of qualities, strengths and weaknesses, in different combinations that characterise good teachers. What these qualities, and their combinations are, in various contexts for learning, understood from various pedagogical perspectives, is the subject of scientific scrutiny.[17] However, all this research does not *create* the perfect teacher, because circumstances evolve, and qualities of people cannot be controlled. All popular memories of good teachers from whom we have learned so much are personal memories, conveying nothing more than personal reveries. Of course, we remember individuals who we considered to be good teachers, sometimes, when they gave us something we needed, told us something we liked to know, maybe even on a regular basis, because they seemed to understand and like us. However, these same individuals were also disliked by some of our fellow classmates, for all kinds of personal reasons.

What we are saying here is this: crucially, good teachers have established a good collaborative working relationship with their students. Claiming, as many people do, that we should merely invest in teachers, or that the teacher is the centre of education, is ignoring completely the collaborative relationships in teaching, and is therefore ignoring the core of the teaching-learning process. Good teachers have an effective working relationship with their students.

In addition, teachers and students together are part of an effective practice characterised by collaborative working relationships facilitating each other. This practice is recognised and supported by school management and communicated and accepted by parents, as far as is possible. Collaborative agency is situated in collaborative structure. And what about the students? Obviously, their role in effective partnerships is crucial, and therefore they need to be taken seriously as partners. This is not the same as 'anything goes' but is quite something else as 'if you want to give learners control, allow them control over stopping, going back, and repeating video, animations, etc., and not the content order of the lesson'.[18] Learner control is about learners developing *agency* for learning and for collaboration, which will surely not evolve with permission to play a video back and forth. Teacher control is about teachers developing agency to support learners within a collaborative relationship, as part of a practice supporting such relationships. The overall aim is to negotiate gaps between students' everyday experiences and on-going socially and scientifically relevant discourses in society.[19] Or, in other words, to enter a dialogue which is open to discuss the different meanings people attribute to phenomena.[20] Both teacher *and* learner agency are among the most neglected and ignored topics in the history of educational and psychological scientific theory and practice.[21] The current tendency of testing and labelling individuals as problematic learners is bad for teacher – as well as for learner-agency.[22] Throughout history, education always had a tendency towards socializing students to become obedient citizens.[23] We can do with more optimistic views.[24] For example, by extending the notion of participation towards outside of the classroom, towards the idea of democratic education.[25]

So, what is the appeal of the individualistic view on humanity and society?

### 3   Individualistic or Collaborative views on Equality and Sharing

A former UK prime minister called Mrs. Margaret Thatcher upheld a clear individualistic view on society. In an interview in *Women's Own* magazine in 1987[26] she claimed:

> They are casting their problems at society. And, you know, there's no such thing as society. There are individual men and women and there are families. And no government can do anything except through people, and people must look after themselves first. It is our duty to look after ourselves and then, also, to look after our neighbours.

Obviously, she did not invent these ideas herself. Samuel Smiles, a nineteenth century author and government reformer from Scotland, produced what has been called his masterpiece *Self Help* (1859)[27] which proclaimed that poverty was caused largely by irresponsible habits. The book became the bible of Victorian liberalism. British 'free trade' policy – the same policy that Thatcher and her imitators fanatically insisted upon – caused the death of almost 2 million out of 8 million Irish subjects in four years, in the period 1845–1849.[28] The doctrine of insisting that people should look after themselves has its basis in individualism, the view that people should only care for their own benefit. The author Ayn Rand, who is said to be the inspiration for the current American president, Donald Trump, formulated this as follows[29]:

> Man – every man – is an end in himself, not a means to the ends of others; he must live for his own sake, neither sacrificing himself to others nor sacrificing others to himself; he must work for his rational self-interest, with the achievement of his own happiness as the highest moral purpose of his life.

It is interesting to note that such individualism often exploits rationality as a desirable feature, and usually treats altruism, compassion, empathy, as food for wimps. The individualistic world needs strong characters, geniuses that stand out in an ocean of mediocrity. Acting rationally means not being concerned with feelings of others, and side-stepping empathy.[30]

Indeed, when politicians, philosophers and economists do not recognise equality as a fundamental value, but instead preach complete individual freedom, their main option is a world with winners and losers. Moreover, if these people do not recognise that even with this option there is a society (or a culture), in which winners can only win because there are losers to exploit, we are denying interdependency, akin to claiming that independent bricks can constitute a house on their own. Not only does each brick have its own function as a constituting element of the building, but also, we need cement to make them stick together. What the individualistic view is proclaiming is a society in which a limited number of winners play around with individual puppets, which should not unite to be strong enough to resist.[31] This not only applies to current neo-liberal societies, especially the views of the US Republican party,[32] but it also looks like the current model of many universities and public administrations in the UK, France, and the Netherlands, and perhaps also in other countries.[33]

FIGURE 12.1  Edward Hicks: The Peaceable Kingdom (1834) (https://commons.wikimedia.org/wiki/File:The_Peaceable_Kingdom_by_Edward_Hicks,_c._1846,_oil_on_canvas_-_De_Young_Museum_-_DSC01288.JPG)

In such individualistic societies and the practices on which they are based, collaboration cannot evolve, because there is no reason for equality, sharing, nor mutual respect in individualistic societies. This has been going on for such a long time, modern society having created stable structures reinforcing assumptions of individualism,[34] that it seems easier to live and accept this rather than to oppose it. An individualistic society cannot be collaborative because there is no equality. But how about sharing ideas? The sociologist Richard Sennett[35] writes about what he calls natural unstable collaboration. The painting "The Peaceable Kingdom" (Figure 12.1) shows the Garden of Eden before aggression, displaying various creatures in a harmonious scene. During the age of Enlightenment, this was the state of nature that we were supposed to return to. But nature is not a stable state, however we define it, because the natural environment is never fixed, things are changing all the time; so cooperation cannot be stable either. For the same reason that social animals collaborate (because they need each other for survival), this collaboration cannot be of one and the same kind (because surviving in a changing environment requires flexibility and interpretation).

Sennett proposes to look for fundamental patterns of give and take, which he calls the 'spectrum of exchange'. All animals figure out kinds of exchange, and five segments of such a spectrum can be distinguished:

> altruistic exchange, which entails self-sacrifice; win-win exchange, in which both parties benefit; differentiating exchange, in which the partners become aware of their differences; zero-sum exchange, in which one party prevails at the expense of another; and winner-takes-all exchange, in which one party wipes out the other ... in human terms, the spectrum runs from Joan of Arc to genocide. (p. 72)

Of these alternatives, only one can be collaborative, and another one may be the highest form of cooperation possible in an individualistic society dominated by corporate interests. The prototypical win-win exchange is the business deal where all parties gain. It requires negotiation skills, perhaps not sticking to all details, and having a perspective of the other as an equal and as someone to be trusted, at least to a sufficient degree, or with sufficient power to counter any threat. There seems to be a lot of collaboration in globalisation, airlines or large companies joining forces, sharing expertise or parts of their production line. But not all business deals may involve collaboration. The business world may not be characterised in terms of trust but rather by caution and alertness. Business deals can be agreed without much respect for the other, and the gains from the other side are a mere by-product of our own gains, an outcome of manipulation.

Only the differentiating exchange, which is in the middle of the spectrum, qualifies as evolving into collaboration. The main reason is mutual respect. With mutual respect, we are open to ideas from others, there is potential learning involved in the interaction: two strangers meet at a bar, talk casually and come away from the encounter with a sharper personal understanding of their own interests, their own desires and their own values. Learning involves relating to others, and the two strangers have developed some relationship that may (or may not) evolve further. This example is interesting, as it does not come from deliberate planning of the participants to learn or develop a relationship, but also it is taking place in an informal setting, which has been designed as a meeting place for this kind of encounters. Just like empathy, or even exploiting empathy, social encounters in a context in which 'Geselligkeit', 'sociabilité' are supported can be the start of mutual understanding and shared action to evolve, even between people who do not know each other very well. This need not naturally or necessarily develop into collaboration, but it could, if the interaction includes respectful mutual awareness of the other person. The lecture-room in colleges, or a man speaking in a Bierhaus to manipulate a crowd, do not qualify, per se, as situations of sharing ideas or developing mutual respect. But we should acknowledge the crucial role of *structure*, as part of evolving practice, for making possible the development of collaboration.

Sharing ideas in collaboration is not striving for everyone to *agree* with *the same* ideas. It refers to the joint effort of equal participants to move some discussion forward by joint contributions and attempts to accommodate to new ideas. A politician speaking at a rally, primarily wants others to agree with his ideas. Actually, in such circumstances, not many people really understand, and that is exactly the purpose of such one-sided sharing attempts. Often, in politics and education alike, there is the authoritarian demand that all share the *correct* idea. Such an idea should also be a *simple* idea. This is called manipulation, which has been exercised in politics up to its most extreme versions.[36] In collaboration, sharing runs both ways, in which case the outcome is learning, not manipulation.

Although there is genuine inequality and injustice at the base of much societal anger, humans have a weak spot for collective, albeit one-sided solutions for their fears and ambitions. Such solutions seem to be easily induced or manipulated, because the effect is that of birds or ants moving into the same direction, seemingly collaborative, arousing some kind of collective pleasure. One of the most horrible and despicable psychological experiments was conducted in the fifties, with two groups of boys, peacefully enjoying themselves in some resort, until researchers installed competition and rivalry. The researchers succeeded in creating aggression and hate, and one group of boys set fire to the other group's dwelling, among other things. The report by the researchers was taken as a standard for the natural tendency of humans towards competition and battle.[37] Despite the researcher's attempts to install conflict twice before, earlier groups of boys became friends,[38] and only a third attempt with different groups led to the satisfactory result for the researchers (the other two attempts were never reported). A schoolteacher who published a novel of fiction about rivalry between boys left on an island turning violent even received the Nobel Prize.[39] Amongst the million possible examples of children who function adequately in small groups, these cases of conflict, supported by malicious research, or complete fiction, seem to receive most attention. History is full of examples of war and conflict, and our society is full of examples of greed and manipulation. This does not prove that we all are like that, nor does it prove that we cannot be collaborators. Some forms of collaboration may come naturally, but others seem to be quite difficult to achieve. We should understand that some types of conflicts and tensions are a natural part of collaboration: for example, we need to learn how to deal with losing face, or with differences in background of any kind, and not take such tensions as issues against collaboration.[40] Collaboration, especially the more interesting and elaborate kind, which is about difficult issues and includes working with people with very different views, always needs to evolve, and can also fail, especially when people are not listening to each other, but only trying to convey their own ideas. Collaboration, literally meaning *working together*, means jointly shaping something new.[41]

Before we discuss some historical and current attempts to install collaborative practices in society, let us first move back (again) to the roots of the idea of social support as a crucial element of society. There is fundamental disagreement on how we are supposed to survive as a species, and within that disagreement, we seem to have lost collaboration as an option.

## 4  The Need for Cooperation

Humans have been described both as highly cooperative animals that need to work hard to keep selfish and aggressive urges under control, and as highly competitive animals that nevertheless can get along and engage in give-and-take. The 19th century geologist and anarchist Peter Kropotkin (Figure 12.2) studied the villages of Siberia, towns and settlements under difficult conditions. He discovered that mutual aid thrived in localities that were furthest removed from population centres. This was not only because of the necessity to work together but also, because of their remote location, making these villages free from the actions of bureaucratic bunglers. Kropotkin stressed the impossibility of doing anything useful for the mass of the people by means of the prevailing administrative machinery. It is the constructive work of the people (and animals) that shapes their society. Evolution favours aggregations of organisms trying to find out the best ways of combining the wants of the individuals with those of co-operation for the welfare of the species.[42]

Thomas Henry Huxley, defending the views of Darwin during the same period, entertained the opposite position (1888), which was that the ethical progress of society depends, not on imitating evolution, still less in running away from it, but in combatting it. Man needed to revolt against an amoral Nature, not to return to it. Huxley had also travelled, and he concluded that life in evolution was a continuous free fight, in which the war of each against all was the normal state of existence. Utter nonsense, Kropotkin argued. Yes, it was true that competition was real, but it was a relatively weak force, and what nature really shows at every turn is that sociability is as much a law of nature as mutual struggle. Kropotkin presents many detailed examples from the animal kingdom, and his favourite species was the ant. Not only do ants display mutual aid, by feeding the ant that has returned from a journey, but they also punish an ant that refuses to dispense aid.

FIGURE 12.2  Peter Kropotkin c. 1900 (aged 57); Thomas Henry Huxley 1874 (aged 49) (https://en.wikipedia.org/wiki/Peter_Kropotkin and https://en.wikipedia.org/wiki/Thomas_Henry_Huxley)

Pure reasoning does not seem to play a major role in human moral decision-making.[43] In the spirit of Kropotkin, the primatologist and productive author Frans de Waal (2011) contends that morality is derived from animal sociality, an idea already proposed by Darwin. We pick up the moods of others, expressed by their body language and facial expressions. Pairs of people who have lived together for a long time not only tend to look more similar after some time, but also show emotional convergence: they easily pick up each other's emotions; the man feels bad when the woman does, and vice-versa. This may have its roots in maternal care of infants, bonding with the mothers making the infant feel safe and happy. In later life, it may look like happiness comes from money, success or fame, but what is better for our well-being is time spent with family and friends.

From the viewpoint of nature, security is the first and foremost reason for social life. Our ancestors needed to stick together to survive. The larger the danger, or the more vulnerable the species, the larger its aggregation. Political leaders know this, and it only takes them to install fear of some enemy, and humans stick together to follow the leader to save them. Of course, we cannot derive the goals of society from the goals of nature. We do not think that society should function according to the laws of nature: society has evolved, as has the role of security, which seems to have different pertinence and shape, depending on the culture and the history of a community. From the viewpoint of evolution, however, our society is not the design of independent men, as it has evolved out of social life. The struggle for existence is not so much one of each against all, as Huxley would claim, but rather of masses of organisms against a hostile environment, as Kropotkin claimed in his 1902 book, *Mutual*

*Aid*. The ability to function in a group and build a support network is a crucial survival skill. Society is not based on love and sympathy, it is based on the unconscious recognition of the force of human solidarity, which is borrowed by each person from the practice of mutual aid – of the close dependency of every one's happiness upon the happiness of all.

For example, chimpanzees show community concern, as when a male chimpanzee settles a female dispute over watermelons by standing between both parties with arms spread out until they stop screaming. This also shows the importance of *roles* of individuals in the community: mediation, disarmament, policing (in the case of chimpanzees). Such roles are not simply altruistic: they also benefit the individual who enacts them. Those who gain from the society are expected to contribute, and conversely, those who contribute feel entitled to get something out of it.

## 5   Collaborative Practices

Mutual aid, consolation or targeted helping may not completely cover the conception of collaboration envisaged in this book. It seems that those concepts deal with mutual support between individuals, or groups of individuals acting for the sake of the same goals. There may be synchronised efforts involved. We know that mutual aid within a group does not preclude hostilities between different groups. Maybe mutual aid is mainly confined to groups in situations of hardship. Kropotkin also discusses mediaeval free cities, in which mutual aid flowed from the guilds of stonemasons, carpenters, merchants, painters, teachers and musicians that coexisted within the walls of the mediaæval city. These cities had freed themselves from the burden of their worldly and clerical lords, a movement taking place all over Europe during the tenth and eleventh centuries. Here arts and crafts flourished, and inductive science took hold. Details on how this actually took place are missing. Eventually, the cities became too big, and conflicts of interest arose between groups within the city. For example, trade, which was formerly communal became the privilege of the merchant and artisan families, and then became subject to individual interests and oppressive trusts.

During his travels to the USA, at the end of the nineteenth century, where his ideas had many supporters, Kropotkin met Booker T. Washington in New York City, and also stayed at Jane Addams' 'Hull House', in Chicago.[44] These were founders of American 'workshops', grass-roots organisations in the spirit of the old social left, for which shared conclusions were not necessary, and collaboration was the goal rather than the means to achieve some end. One does not need to agree in order to collaborate! Hull House, founded by Ellen Gates Starr and Jane Addams in 1889, was a community of people from the streets, combined with other, university-trained residents.[45] They engaged in activities, or not, such as teaching and learning of English. Classrooms were mixed with many kinds of foreigners engaged in a linguistic struggle, playing, discussing, arguing, as they rehearsed the English language. The community organiser tried to engage poor people and losers, focusing on their immediate experiences to recover from passivity. The main staff instruction was to assist, rather than to direct. The idea was to increase solidarity through informality, in an experience of sociability and empathy. Booker T. Washington, a former slave, established two institutions in which African-Americans recovering from slavery could stay and be trained in some skill. By shaping their technical skills in animal husbandry, horticulture, carpentry and metalworking, and teaching them how to teach, these students could spread the skills when they returned home. The workshop was in part individual, but meetings in which the workers discussed their work without the teacher were included. Nevertheless, these institutions, The Tuskegee Institute in Alabama, and the Hampton Agriculture Institute in Virginia, involved a more top-down spirit than the Hull Houses discussed before.

Making a big leap in time, in current society (2019 as we write this), it is not hard to find people joining forces for the sake of a better world. For example, since 2012 there is an important European Union initiative to fund the creation of collaborative platforms for sustainability and grassroots social innovation.[46] Consortia of communities and researchers, including technologists, can propose new projects. Concrete examples include open democracy, open policy-making (based on open data), the collaborative economy, collaborative manufacturing, collaborative consumption patterns and collaborative approaches to inclusion, agriculture, health, and disaster management. While not all projects may evolve into great successes, we are learning about how to exploit collaboration for the sake of a sustainable society. It is these and similar initiatives, involving groups of citizens, and innovative start-up companies, that may warrant some hope about the advent of a more collaborative society. Indeed, it is not the current generation of politicians and policy makers that we look to for views on collaboration in society. Look for initiatives by communities of people who have ideas that go beyond pleasing voters and making money.

Collaboration, throughout history, has been established as a practice in various forms. It also has been installed to achieve other means, such as political purposes. As with all processes, it develops inside practices, and sometimes it is shaped in the form of rituals.[47] A ritual such as *chivalry* was invented for rough knights to engage with (especially) women without immediately raping them; rituals of *courtesy* were meant to make conversation pleasurable for the other. Those were days when it was necessary to explain that it was important to listen to people, and to speak clearly, especially with people one did not know. Civility was developed to be a non-aggressive, respectful, ritualistic way of casual talk, meant to make the other feel good. Not behaving according to the rules of civility caused embarrassment.

It may be that there is an optimal size for groups to collaborate or engage in several forms of constructive activity. This size may also depend on the motives for collaboration. In daily life, opportunities for collaboration are manifold, but often ignored. Many differences between people, or between groups of people, can be overcome, in principle, as soon as we realise that in our global society, differences between people who live in the same area, or are part of the same community are increasing, and that this can be exploited rather than being a source of tension and conflict. The sociologist Sennett (see Endnotes 35 and 46 of this chapter) calls this phenomenon *synoikismos*, the fact that different groups must live together, as it were, in the same house. How to make different minds meet, how to engage in exchanges for mutual benefit? This is where collaboration comes in, in various forms differing in their demands. It is here also that our third dimension enters on the stage: dialogic skills, such as listening well, behaving tactfully, finding and managing disagreement, avoiding frustration. We have seen our poor farmers and samurai working on better understanding each other, especially during the first period of their joint mission. Their collaboration was messy, but at the crucial stage, they had found a collaborative working mode, in which they could respectfully interact and face the common enemy together. At the start, both parties did not trust and understand each other sufficiently. As their collaboration proceeded, they managed to create some openness towards each other. Through such created openings, dialogue started and shared understanding and action emerged.

Sennett (op. cit., pp. 127–129) summarises the point for us as follows:

> Civility made sense of how people in experimental, innovative workshops could best learn from one another, civility as an open, inquisitive discussion about problems, procedures, and results …. In exploring rehearsals and in conversations, we sought some principle that would make cooperation more open. That principle is dialogic cooperation. This kind of cooperation is our goal, our Holy Grail. Dialogic cooperation, entails a special kind of openness, one which enlists empathy rather than sympathy in its service (…). Our social arrangements for cooperation need a

reformation. Modern capitalism has unbalanced competition and cooperation, and so made cooperation in itself less open, less dialogic.

All of this means to say that every aspect of our social behaviour can either be called into question, or can be in the process of evolving into something socially acceptable, creating possibilities to act collaboratively. Collaboration is always under tension, and conditions and structures are subject to change. We need to improvise. In fact, for some, the essence of collaboration is contained in improvisation, as in the case of expert jazz musicians flexibly reacting and adding to each other's musical ideas during the act of playing, without or with minimal planning beforehand.[48] Building on the ideas of others, on the spot is crucial for creative collaboration. The social issue we are discussing in this chapter, individuals considering their own benefits, people imposing ideas on others, or a control structure that constrains what people can do, starts before the creative flow of ideas and activity. We think that sustained collaboration is fundamentally a matter of developing *collaborative agency*, meaning: (1) better understanding various forms of collaboration, and how they relate to existing practices, flexibly related to its goals and participants, (2) developing the attitude of being always open to collaborative possibilities, or turning controlled or scripted activities into collaborative activities, and (3) developing dialogical ways of dealing with other people. Such agency can evolve into a supportive *collaborative structure*, characterised by (1) a practice in which collaboration is allowed to evolve and the knowledge about such developments is shared, (2) respectful relationships between the participants, or the understanding this matters and how to establish such relationships, and (3) a motivation to transform, or evolve, when this is a meaningful possibility.

## 6    Coda

The current times are full of examples of collaboration. We recommend reading R. Keith Sawyer's book on creative collaboration (see endnotes to this chapter), especially in commercial contexts, and taking a closer look at the collaborations between communities, business, politicians and science proposed in the European CAPS framework (Collective Awareness Platforms for sustainable societies), to make us feel optimistic about the already achieved successes. We would like to say that at least some forces in society are moving towards more equality, joint sharing and co-construction, and mutual consideration.

Discussing at the level of society (instead of observing what people actually *do*) makes it difficult to define activities as collaboration. For us to do that, we need to take a closer look at activities we have discussed here. In this chapter, we tried to generalise but could not specify that various collaborative activities indeed have been part of transformative forces in society. This conclusion was not the result of our own research, and instead of looking at things from a coherent theoretical background, we exploited the work of scholars from various disciplinary backgrounds (including sociology, primatology, and history). It then appeared possible to make our point by contrasting two sides – the individualist and the collectivist – in thinking about the collaborative society.

Most people do not seem to learn from history. Instead they realistically adapt to the forces and practices around them. This adaptive capacity allows people to go along with the suddenly changed regime after elections or revolutions, or with the views of populists claiming to have discovered a common enemy.[49] Above, we discussed the dictators and rhetoricians trying to share and impose their views on audiences. Also, we addressed the mechanism from the other side, the side of those adapting to the views of others. Both are two sides of the same coin that represents one-sided sharing, in a system of exchange in which money flows in one direction. We propose to change our currency exchange system to one in which taking something always comes with giving something equally meaningful and relevant in return, transforming the currency into that of collaboration flowing in all directions. As an example: from now on scientific Nobel prizes should be awarded to teams, not individuals.[50]

## Notes

1  Ideas in this paragraph and the next are derived from Dreier (1999).
2  See De Waal (2010).
3  See Sawyer (2007).
4  "Society in its unified and structural character is the fact of the case; the non-social individual is an abstraction arrived at by imagining what man would be if all his human qualities were taken away. Society, as a real whole, is the normal order, and the mass as an aggregate of isolated units is the fiction" (Dewey, 2008, p. 232).
5  See Bohm (2013).
6  The documentary 'Requiem for the American Dream', featuring Noam Chomsky, suggests there are several sources of manipulation of the people by those in power. Those forces are clearly against collaboration and democracy.
7  See Kropotkin (1902/2012, p. 95).
8  See Chomsky and Polychroniou (2017).
9  See Richerson et al. (2016).

10 See Debney (2017) and Klein (2016).
11 On the deskilling of collaboration in current society, Sennett (2012, pp. 7–9) discusses how modern society has weakened collaboration: the dramatic increase of inequality, leading to social distance; the silo-effect, whereby departments and people are isolated within different units; the habit of limiting time that teams work together, which limits their collaboration to evolve; the development of personal tendencies to limit tensions caused by differences, leading to cultural homogenization. All of this leads to de-skilling people in practising collaboration.
12 Admittedly, this is not entirely true: both in the UK and in the Netherlands, for example, visitation committees also evaluate the performance of a whole university department on a regular basis. This allows assessing policies (and allocating funds) instead of individual performance. Also, individual publication records are combined to measure group performance. In other words, actual collaboration is still not addressed.
13 See Tett (2015).
14 See Bereiter (2005).
15 See Ehrenreich (2010).
16 See Zweig (1943/2009). The following quotes from this book picture the situation of schooling in Vienna at the end of the nineteenth century. While this can be read as a caricature by some, some of it (but not all) is still valid for the current situation, and we can see elements returning. Most importantly, in education, we still do not understand how to handle the different roles of the teacher and the student, and therefore cannot see their relationship as collaborative. This is directly related to the role of schools, and of the young, in society. Please consider the following excerpts, especially for its institutional and societal views (all from Chapter 2):

> For, if I am to be honest, the entire period of my schooling was no other than a constant and wearisome boredom, accompanied year after year by an increased impatience to escape from this treadmill. I cannot recall ever having been either "joyous" or "blissful" during that monotonous, heartless, and lifeless schooling which thoroughly spoiled the best and freest period of our existence. I must admit that even today I cannot help experiencing a certain feeling of envy when I see with how much more freedom, happiness, and independence children are permitted to develop in the present century. It still seems hardly credible to me when I observe today how naturally they chat as equals with their teachers, how they hurry to school without a care, whereas we were constantly filled – with a feeling of inadequacy; how they may freely express the desires and inclinations of their young and curious souls both at home and in school – free, independent and natural beings, whereas all of us, as soon as we stepped into the hated building, were forced to cringe lest we strike our foreheads against an invisible yoke. For us school was compulsion, ennui, dreariness, a place where we had to

assimilate the "science of the not-worth-knowing" in exactly measured portions – scholastic or scholastically manufactured material which we felt could have no relation to realty or to our personal interests. It was a dull, pointless learning that the old pedagogy forced upon us, not for the sake of life, but for the sake of learning. And the only truly joyful moment of happiness for which I have to thank my school was the day that I was able to shut the door on it for ever.

... It was not that our Austrian schools were bad in themselves. On the contrary, after a hundred years of experience, the curriculum had been carefully worked out and, had it been transmitted with any inspiration, could have been the basis for a fruitful and fairly universal education. But because of their accurate arrangement and their dry formulary our lessons were frightfully barren and lifeless, a cold teaching apparatus which never adapted itself to die individual, but automatically registered the grades, "good," sufficient," and "insufficient," depending on how far we had complied with the "requirements" of the curriculum. It was exactly this lack of human affection, this empty impersonality and the barracks-like quality of our surroundings, that unconsciously embittered us. We had to learn our lessons and were examined on what we had learned. For eight years no teacher asked us even once what we personally wished to learn, and that encouraging stimulus, for which every young person secretly longs, was totally lacking.

... Nor were our teachers to blame for the dreariness of the institution. They were neither good nor bad; they were not tyrants, nor on the other hand were they helpful comrades, but poor devils who were slavishly bound to the schedule, the officially designated curriculum. They had to accomplish their task as we had to do ours, and – we felt this clearly – they were as happy as we were when in the afternoon the school bell rang and gave them, and us, freedom. They did not love us, they did not hate us, and why should they, for they knew nothing about us ; even after a year or two they knew only a few of us by name. According to the teaching methods of those times, they had nothing to do but to determine how many mistakes we had made in our last lesson. They sat up at their desks and we sat below, they questioned and we had to reply, and there was no other relation between us. For between teacher and pupil, between teacher desk and school bench, the visible above and the visible below, stood the invisible barrier of "authority" which prevented all contact. For a teacher to regard a pupil as an individual (which would have demanded particular attention to the special qualities of the pupil, or the preparation of "reports" or written observations about him, which is a matter of course today) would at that time have exceeded not only the teacher's authority but his capabilities as well. On the other hand, a private conversation would have lessened his authority, for this would have placed the scholars on the same level with him, die superior.

> ... the State exploited the schools as an instrument for the maintenance of its authority. Above all else we were to be educated to respect the existing as perfect, the opinion of the teacher as infallible, our father's words as uncontradictable, the provisions of the State as absolute and valid for all eternity. A second cardinal principle of the pedagogy of those times, which also was applied within the family, directed that young people were not to have things too easy. Before any rights were allowed them they were to learn that they had duties, and above all others the obligation of complete docility. It was to be impressed upon us from the very start that we, who had not yet accomplished anything in life and were entirely without experience, should simply be thankful for all that was granted to us, and had no right to ask or demand anything. In my time this stupid method of intimidation was practised from earliest childhood.

17 See Bruner (1996, chapter 4, "Teaching the present, past, and possible").
18 See De Bruyckere, Kirschner, and Hulshof (2016).
19 See Lemke (1990) and Furberg, and Ludvigsen (2008).
20 See Wegerif (2008).
21 See Matusov, von Duyke, and Kayumova (2016).
22 See Nichols, Berliner, and Noddings (2007).
23 See Alheit (2009).
24 See de Winter (2017).
25 See Engel (2008).
26 See http://www.margaretthatcher.org/document/106689
27 See Smiles (1879).
28 For an economic perspective on the causes of the potato famine, see Mokyr and Gráda (2002). For an Irish political perspective on the potato famine, refer to Gallagher (1995). The horror of what is casually referred to as the 'Potato Famine' is meticulously chronicled in *The Great Hunger: Ireland 1845–1849*, by Cecil Woodham-Smith (1962). The first paragraphs set the tone:
> At the beginning of 1845, the state of Ireland was as it had been for nearly seven hundred years, a source of grave anxiety to England. Ireland had first been invaded in 1169; it was now 1845 yet she had been neither assimilated nor subdued. The country had been invaded not once but several times, the land had been conquered and redistributed over and over again, the population had been brought to the verge of extinction – after Cromwell's conquest and settlement only some half million Irish survived – yet an Irish nation still existed, separate, numerous and hostile. The population had increased during the period following the rape of Ireland by Cromwell in 1649, to 8 million in 1845. It was during Cromwell's war on Ireland that an estimated 40% of the land was confiscated and transferred to the ownership of the English Nobility. Two hundred years later the population of Ireland was poor, landless and 3 million Irish are said to

have subsisted on a diet of potatoes alone. The blessing, and the curse, of the potato is that it is nearly the perfect food and with a wee bit of milk, it is possible to live a healthy life on the potato alone. The Potato Blight made its appearance in 1845 and by 1846 had destroyed the Potato Crop. As 1847 arrived, three million souls were in immediate danger of death by starvation. The blow dealt by blight was followed by the monstrous actions of the land-owning aristocrats, the majority of whom lived their lives of luxury in England funded by rents extracted annually from the Irish Celt. The land owners were estimated to have caused the eviction of a half million Gaels from their homes during the famine years. The combination of famine and homelessness led to the unspeakable deaths of one million Celtic souls, many dying in road side ditches.

29 See Rand (1962).
30 See Bloom (2016).
31 See Marx (2008).
32 See https://www.youtube.com/watch?v=KNbgZjMVkqg; https://youtu.be/-UNDu-APMAuw
33 As an example, in the Netherlands there is ongoing debate about financing the care for the elderly generation, say people over 65, although the age is moving up. A system of homes for the elderly was established in the fifties of the 20th century, free for those who could not afford it. For those with some money it was better to get rid of that money before moving to an elderly house, because they had to pay for it. The point is, that based on the solidarity principle all elderly persons were treated equally: all were entitled to have a place in an elderly home. Nowadays, in 2017, elderly homes have been replaced with personal day-care, tuned to the individual needs of the elder person. This is a more individualised system, leading to many individual issues. The budget has been transferred from national to municipal responsibilities, and day-care is privatised, so there are ruthless time-constraints and a huge administrative load for day-care workers. Individuals with money prefer to buy private care, and some well networked elderly people are getting organised to go and live in large houses together and pay for the care they need. As a consequence, some individuals benefit, while others have a lot to complain. Individual complaints are less powerful and can easily be dismissed. There also is a new type of complaint, typical for current times, although applicable to the situation in the previous century as well: why should those elderly that have a lot of money pay for those who do not have any money left in the bank because they spent it on liquor and women? We may try and answer that question, but what is revealing lies behind the question itself: where has solidarity gone? The reasoning in a me-first society differs from that of a collaborative society, although the nature of some of the problems may be similar.
34 An interesting note comes from nanobiology, where the notion of individual (meaning: *indivisible*) is being challenged. What is seen as an individual can also be

understood as a temporary crossing of genetic evolutionary trajectories and those of metabolic processes at the level of the cells. In addition, biotechnical interventions can also change 'individuals' (Dupré, 2010).

35 The next three paragraphs are based on Sennett (2012, chapter 2).
36 "Get me Roger Stone": A documentary exploring the life and career of notorious Republican dirty trickster and long-time Trump advisor, Roger Stone, who helped create the real-estate mogul's political career. See also http://www.newyorker.com/news/ryan-lizza/trumps-good-job-call-to-roger-stone
37 See Sherif (1961).
38 See Perry (2014).
39 We are referring here to the work of fiction by William Golding, *Lord of the Flies* (1954), about a group of boys who ended up on an island. The main message of the novel can be summarised as: "I must say that anyone who moved through those years without understanding that man produces evil as a bee produces honey, must have been blind or wrong in the head." Apparently, the 1983 Nobel Prize Committee, represented by professor Lars Gyllensten agrees with this contention (https://www.nobelprize.org/nobel_prizes/literature/laureates/1983/presentation-speech.html)
40 See Andriessen, Baker, and van der Puil (2010).
41 See Bohm (2013).
42 See Kropotkin (1902/2012).
43 See De Waal (2010), Norenzayan et al. (2016) and Tomasello (2016).
44 See Dugatkin (2011).
45 Based on Sennett (2012, chapter 2).
46 See https://ec.europa.eu/digital-single-market/sites/digital-agenda/files/focus_16_accessibility.pdf
47 Ideas in this and the next paragraph are again based on the book by Richard Sennett (2012).
48 See Sawyer (2007).
49 See Snyder (2016).
50 See Bliss (1992).

## References

Alheit, P. (2009). Biographical learning – within the new lifelong learning discourse. In K. Illeris (Ed.), *Contemporary theories of learning* (pp. 116–128). New York, NY: Routledge.

Andriessen, J., & Baker, M., & van der Puil, C. (2010). Socio-cognitive tension in collaborative working relations. In S. R. Ludvigsen, A. Lund, I. Rasmussen, & R. Säljö (Eds.), *Learning across sites: New tools, infrastructures and practices*. London: Routledge.

Bereiter, C. (2005). *Education and mind in the knowledge age*. London: Routledge.
Bliss, M. (1992). *Banting: A biography*. Toronto: University of Toronto Press.
Bloom, P. (2016). *Against empathy*. New York, NY: Ecco.
Bohm, D. (2013). *On dialogue*. London: Routledge.
Bruner, J. S. (1996). *The culture of education*. Cambridge, MA: Harvard University Press.
Chomsky, N., & Polychroniou, C. J. (2017). *Optimism over despair*. London: Penguin.
Debney, B. (2017). Historical nature versus nature in general: Capitalism in the web of life. *Capitalism Nature Socialism, 28*(2), 126–131.
De Bruyckere, P., Kirschner, P. A., & Hulshof, C. D. (2016). Technology in education: What teachers should know. *American Educator, 40*(1), 12–18.
De Waal, F. (2010). *The age of empathy: Nature's lessons for a kinder society*. New York, NY: Broadway Books.
Dewey, J. (2008). The ethics of democracy. In *The early works of John Dewey, volume 1, 1882–1898: Early essays and Leibniz's new essays, 1882–1888* (J. A. Boydston & G. E. Axetell, Eds.). Carbondale, IL: Southern Illinois University Press.
De Winter, M. (2017, May). *Pedagogiek over hoop. Het onmiskenbare belang van optimisme in opvoeding en onderwijs* [*Pedagogy about hope (pedagogy in a mess). The crucial need for optimism in pedagogy and education*]. Rede ter gelegenheid van het afscheid als Faculteitshoogleraar Maatschappelijke opvoedingsvraagstukken aan de Universiteit Utrecht.
Dreier, O. (1999). Personal trajectories of participation across contexts of social practice. *Outlines. Critical Practice Studies, 1*(1), 5–32.
Dugatkin, L. A. (2011). The prince of evolution: Peter Kropotkin's adventures in science and politics. *CreateSpace*, 80–81.
Dupré, J. (2010). The polygenomic organism. *The Sociological Review, 58*(Suppl. 1), 19–31. https://doi.org/10.1111/j.1467-954X.2010.01909.x
Ehrenreich, B. (2010). *Smile or die: How positive thinking fooled America and the world*. London: Granta Books.
Engel, L. H. (2008). Experiments in democratic education: Dewey's lab school and Korczak's children's republic. *The Social Studies, 99*(3), 117–121. https://doi.org/10.3200/TSSS.99.3.117-121
Furberg, A., & Ludvigsen, S. (2008). Students' meaning-making of socio-scientific issues in computer mediated settings: Exploring learning through interaction trajectories. *International Journal of Science Education, 30*(13), 1775–1799. https://doi.org/10.1080/09500690701543617
Gallagher, P. (1995). *How British free trade starved millions during Ireland's Potato Famine*. Washington, DC: The Schiller Institute. Retrieved from https://www.schillerinstitute.org/economy/nbw/pot_famine95.html#links
Golding, W. (1954). *Lord of the flies*. London: Faber & Faber.

Huxley, T. H. (1888). The struggle for existence: A programme. *The Nineteenth Century and After: A Monthly Review, 23*(132), 161–180.

Klein, N. (2016). Let them drown. The violence of othering in a warming world. *London Review of Books, 38*(11), 11–14.

Kropotkin, P. (2012). *Mutual aid: A factor of evolution*. North Chelmsford, MA: Courier Corporation. (Original published 1902)

Lemke, J. L. (1990). *Talking science: Language, learning, and values*. Norwood, NJ: Albex.

Marx, K. (2008). *Das Kapital*. London: John Wiley & Sons, Inc. (Original published xxx)

Matusov, E., von Duyke, K., & Kayumova, S. (2016). Mapping concepts of agency in educational contexts. *Integrative Psychological and Behavioral Science, 50*(3), 420–446. https://doi.org/10.1007/s12124-015-9336-0

Mokyr, J., & Gráda, C. Ó. (2002). What do people die of during famines: The Great Irish Famine in comparative perspective. *European Review of Economic History, 6*(3), 339–363. https://doi.org/10.1017/S1361491602000163

Nichols, S. L., Berliner, D. C., & Noddings, N. (2007). *Collateral damage: How high-stakes testing corrupts America's schools*. Cambridge: Cambridge University Press.

Norenzayan, A., Shariff, A. F., Gervais, W. M., Willard, A. K., McNamara, R. A., Slingerland, E., & Henrich, J. (2016). The cultural evolution of prosocial religions. *Behavioral and Brain Sciences, 39*, e1.

Perry, G. (2014, November). The views from the boys. *The Psychologist, 27*, 834–837.

Rand, A. (1962). Introducing objectivism. *The Objectivist Newsletter, 1*(1), 35.

Richerson, P., Baldini, R., Bell, A. V., Demps, K., Frost, K., Hillis, V., ... Ross, C. (2016). Cultural group selection plays an essential role in explaining human cooperation: A sketch of the evidence. *Behavioral and Brain Sciences, 39*.

Sawyer, R. K. (2007). *Group genius: The creative power of collaboration*. New York, NY: Basic Books.

Sennett, R. (2012). *Together: The rituals, pleasures and politics of cooperation*. New Haven, CT: Yale University Press.

Sherif, M. (1961). *The Robbers Cave experiment: Intergroup conflict and cooperation*. Middletown, CT: Wesleyan University Press.

Smiles, S. (1879). *Self-help: With illustrations of conduct and perseverance*. London: J. Murray.

Snyder, T. (2016). *Black earth: The Holocaust as history and warning*. New York, NY: Tim Duggan Books.

Tett, G. (2015). *The silo effect: The peril of expertise and the promise of breaking down barriers*. New York, NY: Simon and Schuster.

Tomasello, M. (2016). *A natural history of human morality*. Cambridge, MA: Harvard University Press.

Wegerif, R. (2008). Dialogic or dialectic? The significance of ontological assumptions in research on educational dialogue. *British Educational Research Journal, 34*(3), 347–361. https://doi.org/10.1080/01411920701532228

Woodham-Smith, C. (1962). *The great hunger: Ireland, 1845–1849*. London: Hamish Hamilton.

Zweig, S. (2009). *The world of yesterday: Memoirs of a European*. London: Pushkin Press. (Original published 1943)

CHAPTER 13

# Aftermath

Collaboration operates in an arena of tension. Interacting with others leads to encountering their limitations that can be experienced as barriers. Dealing with these limitations, looking for some of the assets, are two dimensions of collaboration that may prevent individuals from engaging with it altogether. Possible extremes, avoiding tension, render operating within the broad middle ground very difficult.

We have experienced collaboration in this book, often as a challenge, as a risk. We defined collaboration as engaging with others, as equals, with a joint purpose, and with sufficient consideration for where the others come from and what they are proposing. Individuals have the freedom to either avoid such tension, or to engage and face some degree of failure together with some degree of accomplishment. Collaboration involves transcending individual limitations on the interpersonal plane.

Collaboration is not only for the purpose of meeting a challenge. It is the more natural way of relating to others and to the world. It involves looking at the whole instead of beginning from an individualistic perspective. We relate to each other, depend on each other; everything we know and do has been evolving in contexts with others. Creativity comes from relating to others. What we propose, also for education, is for people to engage in collaborative relationships, to work on the common grounds in which dealing with others sets the constraints of the group, and at the same time evolving the understanding of how to better relate and expand the possibilities of the group within the context of the world we live in. Collaboration is more than a dialogue: it probably has more constraints, set by the objectives, the participants, the understanding, and the desirability of expanding these constraints. Collaboration is more about action, in addition to talking, reflection or thinking. It is one important way, and not the only one, to evolve our understanding of ourselves in the world of others.

In this book we have made all this personal, to try and provide the reader with multiple perspectives, opening up the concept of collaboration for getting a better place in the reader's personal world.

CHAPTER 13

# Aftermath

Collaboration operates in an arena of tension. Interacting with others leads to encountering their limitations that can be experienced as barriers. Dealing with these limitations, looking for some of the assets, are two dimensions of collaboration that may prevent individuals from engaging with it altogether. Possible extremes, avoiding tension, render operating within the broad middle ground very difficult.

We have experienced collaboration in this book, often as a challenge, as a risk. We defined collaboration as engaging with others, as equals, with a joint purpose, and with sufficient consideration for where the others come from and what they are proposing. Individuals have the freedom to either avoid such tension, or to engage and face some degree of failure together with some degree of accomplishment. Collaboration involves transcending individual limitations on the interpersonal plane.

Collaboration is not only for the purpose of meeting a challenge. It is the more natural way of relating to others and to the world. It involves looking at the whole instead of beginning from an individualistic perspective. We relate to each other, depend on each other; everything we know and do has been evolving in contexts with others. Creativity comes from relating to others. What we propose, also for education, is for people to engage in collaborative relationships, to work on the common grounds in which dealing with others sets the constraints of the group, and at the same time evolving the understanding of how to better relate and expand the possibilities of the group within the context of the world we live in. Collaboration is more than a dialogue: it probably has more constraints, set by the objectives, the participants, the understanding, and the desirability of expanding these constraints. Collaboration is more about action, in addition to talking, reflection or thinking. It is one important way, and not the only one, to evolve our understanding of ourselves in the world of others.

In this book we have made all this personal, to try and provide the reader with multiple perspectives, opening up the concept of collaboration for getting a better place in the reader's personal world.